Calendar of Knights; Containing Lists of Knights Bachelors, British Knights of Foreign Orders, Also Knights of the Garter, Thistle Bath, St. Patrick and the Guelphic and Ionian Orders: From 1760 to the Present Time

Francis Townsend

CALENDAR OF KNIGHTS;

CONTAINING LISTS OF

KNIGHTS BACHELORS,

BRITISH KNIGHTS OF FOREIGN ORDERS,

ALSO KNIGHTS OF THE

GARTER, THISTLE, BATH, ST. PATRICK,

AND THE

GUELPHIC AND IONIAN ORDERS,

FROM 1760 TO THE PRESENT TIME.

BY

FRANCIS TOWNSEND,

PURSUIVANT OF ARMS.

LONDON:
WILLIAM PICKERING.
MDCCCXXVIII.

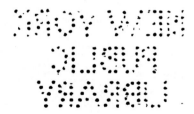
LONDON:
PRINTED BY S. AND R. BENTLEY,
Dorset Street, Fleet Street.

PREFACE.

THE want which, in the course of his professional pursuits, the Editor has repeatedly felt, of some work which should identify, at least, the professions, residences, subsequent honours, if any, and times of death, of persons on whom the honour of knighthood had been conferred, first led him to commence, for his own private use, a Collection on that subject, the more modern (as the more immediately interesting) portion of which he here ventures to offer to the Public, in the hope that it may facilitate the researches of others in a branch of study now becoming daily more and more followed.

While the Peerage and Baronetage of Great Britain and Ireland have been the subjects of numerous, and, of late years, nearly annual publications, the Order of Knighthood has been almost entirely neglected. In fact, the only Work that is confined to that subject, is a List of Knights edited as far back as 1660, by John Philpot, Somerset Herald.   Previous to that period a "Catalogue of Nobility, Baronets and *Knights*," had been published by Thomas Walkley, 1642, a third edition of which, (said to have been collected by Sir Richard St. George, Clarenceux King of Arms,) was printed in 1652.   Lists of the (then) existing Knights have from time to time been given in "Chamberlain's State of England," and some similar works, and more recently in the Appendixes to the several Editions of "Debrett's Peerage and Baronetage."

All these Lists, however, have been more or less defective.   Those of Walkley and Philpot, though embracing all the Knights made within a given period, contain nothing but the mere Names of the parties, the Counties where they resided, and the Dates of their Knighthood ; no attempt being made to record either any further honour to which they may have been advanced, or the dates of their deaths.   All the subsequent Lists profess to contain only the Names of then existing Knights.

Towards the end of the seventeenth century Peter

Le Neve, Esq. Norroy King of Arms, appears to have contemplated the publication of a List of Knights from the Restoration down to his own time; which, to judge from the large collections he had made, (now in the British Museum, Harl. MSS. 5801 and 2,) would probably have contained not only all the particulars that came to his knowledge relative to the several knights themselves, but also valuable genealogical accounts of their families. His death, however, prevented the intended publication.

An extract from the sketch of a Preface, which is to be found in the first volume of Le Neve's Collection, may perhaps not be unacceptable to the reader. After noticing the above-mentioned publications of Philpot and Walkley as the only ones known to him, and stating that he proposed to commence his own List from the 1st of King Charles II. (where the previous work ended,) Le Neve proceeds :—

" The Catalogue I have transcribed from the entries
" thereof in the Heralds' Office, London, which are
" transmitted to them when their fees are paid to the
" Receivour; so that those gentlemen who paid no fees
" must not expect to have any notice taken of the times

" of. their being knighted. But some few who have
" not paid fees, which could any way come to my
" hand, I have added in their due places; and if any
" should be omitted who paid their fees, or any wrong
" dates put to those who are inserted, I ·must beg their
" pardon for the neglect, and shall always be ready
" to amend whatever error I have committed."

The present Editor has drawn from the same source
as his Predecessor, with the addition of the London
Gazettes, in which also the knighthoods of all persons
where fees are paid are notified. Considering also
that, although the notification and record of a knighthood were contingent on the payment of fees, the
knighthood itself is completely conferred the moment
the royal sword has been imposed,* he has inserted in

* This is so completely the case, that it may be doubted whether even a person who should succeed in surreptitiously procur-
ing the *imposition of the sword* from the Sovereign, would be at
all the less a Knight Bachelor on account of the fraud or misre-
presentation he had practised to obtain it.

Two instances of this nature did actually occur about seven
years ago, which led to the following notice in the London Gazette of 5 May, 1821.

" Carlton House, 4 May, 1821.

" The following is a Copy of an Order from His Majesty to
the Marquess of Winchester, Groom of the Stole, which, in,

his List the Names of all such persons as, either from his own knowledge or credible information, he believes to have actually received the honour of knighthood, though they are not included in the records of the College of Arms, or the Gazette, distinguishing, however, such instances with the remark, "Not gazetted."

In the List of Knights Bachelors the description immediately following the Name of the Knight is that which applied to him at the period when he received

obedience to His Majesty's commands, has been communicated by his Lordship to the Lords of His Majesty's Bedchamber.

"The honour of Knighthood having, in two recent instances, been surreptitiously obtained at the levee, His Majesty, for the purpose of effectually guarding against all such disgraceful practices in future, has been pleased to direct, that henceforth no person shall be presented to His Majesty at the levee by the Lord in waiting, to receive the honour of Knighthood, unless His Majesty's pleasure shall have been previously signified, in writing, to the Lord in waiting, by one of His Majesty's principal Secretaries of State."

The names of the parties are not unknown to the Editor, but they are, of course, not included in the following List; and, although they are hinted at in the Gentleman's Magazine at the period, he forbears to mention them here, because one of them is since dead, and the other, he trusts, either has had, or will have, the decency to lay down his surreptitiously obtained title.

the honour; the date of knighthood immediately follows, and the Editor has then added any further rank
or dignity to which the individual may have been
raised, and finally, if dead, the date of his death.*

The honour of Knighthood is sometimes conferred
by Letters Patent under the Great Seal, but only in
cases where the individual on whom His Majesty is
pleased to confer it is out of the kingdom.

The Statutes of the Ionian Order declare, that all
persons who may be admitted into it shall immediately be entitled to assume " the distinctive appellation of Knighthood."

King James I. by Letters Patent, dated 28 May, in
the tenth year of his reign, (about a twelvemonth
after the foundation of the Order of Baronets,) pro-
mised and granted, " for Himself, his Heirs, and Successors, that such Baronets, and the heirs male of
their bodies, as hereafter should be no knights when
they should attain or be of the age of one-and-twenty
years, upon knowledge thereof given to the Lord

* There are probably some deceased persons in the List whose
deaths the Editor has not been able to ascertain, but he believes
the instances are not numerous.

Chamberlain of the Household, should be knighted by His Majesty, his Heirs, and Successors." This promise and grant, however, were revoked and annulled by other Letters Patent, dated 19 Dec. 1827.

All persons on whom His Majesty may be pleased to confer any of the Orders of Knighthood, must be previously made Knights Bachelors,* except Commanders of the Bath, who take the rank of Knights and appellation " Sir," immediately on their nomination, and are, if necessary, subsequently knighted when invested with the Insignia of their class.

FOREIGN ORDERS.

Previous to the year 1800 the instances of Foreign Orders of Knighthood being conferred on English subjects were of so unfrequent occurrence as to excite little attention, either on the part of the Public or the Government. The permission of the British Sovereign was, of course, always necessary to legitimatise the acceptance of a Foreign Order, or authorise the wearing its Insignia in this country; but, even for many

* They are not, however, included in the List of *Knights Bachelors*, as they will be found under their respective Orders.

years subsequent to the accession of His late Majesty, there does not appear to have been any established rule or etiquette as to the mode in which that permission was to be announced or recorded. In some instances His Majesty himself, at the request of the Foreign Sovereign, invested the Knight. In the case of Sir John Hill, M.D. Knight of Gustavus Vasa, all that is known is, that immediately after his investiture, which was performed by the Swedish Ambassador in London, he was received and recognised, at the levee of his own Sovereign, as a Knight of that Order. In another instance, the Royal Permission is said to have been notified by a private letter from the Secretary of State for the Home Department. In the case of Sir Samuel Greig, in 1778, (p. 90,) a certificate from the Lords of the Russian Admiralty, setting forth the Orders which the Emperor of Russia had conferred upon him, was registered in the College of Arms, on the authority of the Earl Marshal's Warrant only; And the only official record of the late Lord Macartney having received the White Eagle of Poland, is a Pedigree of his Lordship's family recorded in the same College.

In 1789, for the first time, the Royal Permission was signified (in the cases of Bentham, p. 71, and Fanshaw, p. 88) by Warrant, under the Signet and Sign Manual. Similar Warrants passed for Lord Duncan (p. 85) in 1797, and for Sir Sidney Smith (p. 54) in 1799; and from that period such has continued to be the uniform practice.

After 1800 the number of Foreign Orders bestowed on British subjects increased immensely. It is a feature of the late War, not perhaps much known, though peculiarly honourable to the British Nation, that the achievements of her Naval and Military Officers not only obtained them admission into the already existing Orders of almost every country in Europe, but even gave rise to the establishment of three new Orders of Knighthood, principally, if not solely, for the purpose of rewarding their services.

The Porte, before 1800, possessed no Order of Chivalry; those already established in the stricter Catholic countries, "being united with religious ceremonies and institutions,"* could not correctly be bestowed on persons professing a different faith. But the Navy and

* Preamble to the Statutes of the Tower and Sword.

Army of Great Britain expelled the French from Naples (1798) and Egypt, (1801,) and protected (1808) the King of Portugal in his removal to the Brazils. The gratitude of the Sultan was shown by the establishment of the Order of the Crescent, and that of the Kings of Naples and Portugal, by their respectively founding the Orders of St. Ferdinand and Merit, and the Tower and Sword.

The strictness of interpretation, however, which would exclude Protestants, was afterwards dispensed with, and the Insignia of most of the Catholic Orders of Spain, Portugal, and Italy, are now to be seen adorning the breasts of British Officers.

Up to the year 1810, it appears to have been generally considered, and acted upon, though nowhere perhaps absolutely decided, that the acceptance of a Foreign Order of Knighthood, (with the consent of the British Sovereign,) gave a title to the appellation " Sir," and the other privileges, rank, and precedence, of a Knight Bachelor of these Realms.

In some instances, where His Majesty personally invested the Knight with the Insignia of the Order bestowed upon him, he at the same time ceremoni-ously dubbed him with the sword. But the appella-tion "Sir" was equally and with as little question, assumed by, and, even in official documents, given to, those who had been created by Diploma only, and had never been actually knighted.

In 1810 the question as to the propriety of this practice was raised, in the case of Sir Henry Cle-ments Thompson, Captain R.N. who had received, with his Sovereign's consent, the Order of the Sword of Sweden, but was appointed by the Lords of the Admiralty to the command of a ship by the descrip-tion of " Henry Clements Thompson, *Esquire.*" The case was referred for the consideration of the Heralds' College, where the opinions were much divided, but the majority decided to report, that the acceptance of a Foreign Order, under such circumstances, did *not* confer the title or rank contended for.

It is the less necessary to state or to combat here, either the grounds of this opinion, or the peculiar fea-tures of the case upon which it was delivered, inasmuch as the direct contrary had been previously *ruled* by the highest legal authority of the kingdom, though the case in which it occurred, being one of assault only, had not come to the knowledge of either the parties or the referees, and is not reported.*

It may be remarked, however, that although Captain Thompson immediately laid down the title, and the Admiralty acted upon the opinion, in the Army Lists, persons similarly circumstanced continued to be called " Sir."

In 1813, a regulation was adopted, that in all future Royal Warrants authorising the acceptance of Foreign Orders, a clause should be inserted providing " that such Licence should not authorise the

---

* It was a prosecution against William Dearsley, for an assault on the Rev. Sir Robert Peat. The Counsel for the defendant took an objection to the description of the plaintiff, urging, that as he had not been knighted by the King he had no right to the appellation " Sir." Lord Ellenborough overruled the objection, on the ground that knighthood was an universal honour, which there could be no doubt every sovereign could confer according to the laws or customs of his own state; and that there could be as little doubt that the King of England could ratify and confirm such creation by a foreign Sovereign, and that having so done, the party was, to all intents and purposes, a Knight, and entitled to the appellation by which Knights are commonly distinguished in these Realms.

assumption of any Style, Appellation, Precedence, or Privilege, appertaining to a Knight Bachelor of these Realms."

It may now, therefore, be laid down as a principle, that *previous to the Regulation of* 1813, the investiture with a Foreign Order, with the permission of His Majesty, intitled the party to the rank, appellation, and privileges, of a Knight Bachelor.

Regulations of His Majesty and of His Royal Highness the Prince Regent, respecting Foreign Orders.

1st. "THAT no British subject shall accept a Foreign Order, or wear its Insignia, without having previously obtained a Warrant under the Royal Sign Manual, (directed to the Earl Marshal of England,) granting them His Majesty's permission to accept and wear the same.

2d. "That the intention of a Foreign Sovereign to decorate a British subject with the Insignia of such Order, shall be notified to His Majesty's Principal Secretary of State for Foreign Affairs, either through the King's Minister abroad, or through the accredited

Minister of the Foreign Sovereign resident at this Court.

3d. " That when His Majesty's Principal Secretary of State for Foreign Affairs shall have taken His Majesty's pleasure, and obtained His consent upon the occasion, he shall then signify the same to His Majesty's Principal Secretary of State for the Home Department, in order that he may cause the usual Warrant to be prepared for the Royal Sign Manual, and take such other steps as may be necessary for carrying His Majesty's pleasure into effect accordingly.

4th. " That when the Warrant is signed by the King, it shall be announced in the Gazette in the usual manner, and registered in His Majesty's College of Arms."

In addition to the above Regulations of the King, His Royal Highness the Prince Regent deemed it expedient to announce, in the year 1812,

5th. " That no subject of His Majesty could be allowed to accept the Insignia of a Foreign Order from any Sovereign of a Foreign State, except they shall be so conferred in consequence of active and distinguished services before the Enemy, either at Sea or in the Field ; or unless he shall have been actually employed in the service of such Foreign Sovereign."

And in March 1813, His Royal Highness was pleased to command, that the following proviso should be thereafter inserted in all Royal Warrants for the acceptance of Foreign Orders :*

6th. "That His Majesty's Licence and Permission doth not authorise, and shall not be deemed or construed to authorise, the assumption of any style, appellation, rank, precedence, or privilege, appertaining unto a Knight Bachelor of these Realms."

N. B. Before the Principal Secretary of State for Foreign Affairs takes the Prince Regent's pleasure, on any application for an Officer in the Army to be permitted to accept a Foreign Order, he causes the same to be referred to the Commander-in-Chief, through His Royal Highness's Secretary, to know whether or not His Royal Highness sees any objection to the Prince Regent's pleasure being taken thereupon.

And if the application be in favour of a Naval

---

* This regulation, when referred to in the Work, has been erroneously called the regulation of 1812.

b

Officer, the Principal Secretary of State for Foreign Affairs communicates with the First Lord of the Admiralty, to the same effect, previous to the Prince Regent's pleasure being taken thereon.

Further Regulation.

" No British Officer to be recommended to the Prince Regent for the honour of Knighthood in consideration of his having received the Royal permission to accept and wear the Insignia of a Foreign Order, unless such Officer shall have attained the rank of Major General in the Army, or of Rear Admiral in the Navy.

" (Signed) CASTLEREAGH."

The List of Knights of Foreign Orders given in this Work may be divided into Three Classes.

I. Persons who have received the Royal Licence to accept them ; in which case the date of such Licence immediately follows the name of the Order; and when the Licence has been duly recorded in the College of Arms, a dagger is prefixed.   When the dagger is not, it is to be concluded the Licence has not been recorded.

II. Officers to whom his Grace ·the Duke of Wellington distributed the Orders which were placed at his disposition by the Allied Sovereigns, after the Battle of Waterloo. These are distinguished by the letter 𝔚. Very few of these Officers have received Royal Licences permitting their acceptance of them, and consequently are not included in the List of British Officers having Foreign Orders, printed in the authorised Army List.*

III. Persons whom though they have not obtained the Royal permission to wear the Insignia in England, the Editor, either of his own knowledge or as matter of historic fact, knows to have received any Foreign Order. This Class, comparatively very small, is to be distinguished by no date following the name of the Order they have received.

To give any thing like a detailed account of the several Foreign Orders of Knighthood which have

---

* It appears singular, that on so distinguished an occasion some general permission did not issue. On a less important one (the conquest of Egypt) general orders from the Commander-in-Chief permitted all officers who had received the Order of the Crescent to wear its Insignia.

been conferred on British subjects, would far exceed the limits of the present Work; the following slight notices, however, may not be unacceptable.

ANNUNCIATION, (*Sardinia*.) Founded by Amadeus VIII. Duke of Savoy, 1434.

CHARLES III. or The IMMACULATE CONCEPTION, (*Spain*.) Founded by Charles III. King of Spain, 1771. Four Classes — Grand Crosses, Commanders, Knights Pensioners, and Knights. This Order ranks immediately after the Golden Fleece, and takes precedence of the much older Orders of Calatrava, Alcantara, St. James, Montera.

CHRIST, (*Portugal.*) Instituted 1319, and endowed with the estates which the then recently suppressed Order of the Templars held in Portugal.

CRESCENT, (*Turkey*.) Founded in August 1799, to reward Lord Nelson, &c. Two Classes.

N.B. The Second Class was conferred at the close of the Egyptian campaign, 1801, on above 800 English officers, but the Editor has not hitherto been able to collect any thing like a correct list of them. Any information on this point will be most thankfully received.

BLACK EAGLE, (*Prussia*.) Founded by Frederick I. King of Prussia, 1701. One Class.

RED EAGLE, (*Prussia.*) Founded by George Frederick Charles Margrave of Brandenburg Bayreuth, 1734, and re-organized by the Margrave of Brandenburg Anspach, 1774. In 1792 the King of Prussia declared himself Grand Master, and ranked it among the Prussian Orders next after the Black Eagle. Three Classes. The Knights of the Black Eagle are also Knights of the First Class of this Order.

WHITE EAGLE, (*Poland.*) Said to have been founded by Uladislaus, King of Poland, 1325, but did not exist many years. Renewed by Augustus King of Poland, 1705.

ELEPHANT, (*Denmark.*) Founded by King Canute IV. 1190, and revived by Christian I. 1458.

GOLDEN FLEECE, (*Austria and Spain.*) This illustrious Order, considered at present the first in rank both in Austria and Spain, was founded in 1429, by Philip the Good, Duke of Burgundy and Earl of Flanders, and the Grand Mastership attached to the Earldom of Flanders. At present the Emperor of Austria and King of Spain, each within their own dominions, exercise the function of Grand Master, and nominate Knights of this Order.

GUSTAVUS VASA, (*Sweden.*) Founded by King Frederick I. about 1725.

IRON CROWN, (*Italy.*) Founded by Napoleon as King of Italy, 1805, for civil as well as military services, and adopted by the Emperor Francis. Three Classes—the first limited to Twenty, the second to Thirty, and the last to Fifty Members.

LEOPOLD, (*Austria.*) Founded by the Emperor Francis II. about 1808, for civil as well as military merit. Three Classes—Grand Crosses, Commanders, and Knights.

LION AND SUN, (*Persia.*) Founded by Futty Ali Shah, 1808, to confer on Foreign Ambassadors, &c. Mussulmen are not admissible. Three Classes.

LEGION of HONOR, (*France.*) Founded by Napoleon, 1802, and confirmed by Louis XVIII. 1814. Five Classes—Grand Crosses, (formerly called Grand Cordon, or Grand Aigle,) 140; Grand Officers, 240; Commanders, 650; Officers, 2000; Knights, unlimited.*

MALTA, or ST. JOHN of JERUSALEM. The general history of this celebrated Order (the Patriarch of European chivalry) is too well known to need recapitulation. It is only necessary to say here, that after flourishing for many centuries in the Holy Land, at Cyprus, at Rhodes,

---

* In 1813 this Class amounted to 39,200, and it has been since much increased.

and finally, in the Island from which its more modern designation is taken, its existence as a sovereign state was put an end to by Buonaparte, who reduced the Island and expelled the Knights, in his passage towards Egypt in 1798. A majority of the Knights then retired to Trieste, and afterwards to Messina and Catana. At present the Order is under the protection of the Emperor of Russia.

MARIA-THERESA, (*Austria.*) Founded 1757, by the Empress whose name it bears. Consists of three Classes—Grand Crosses, Commanders, and Knights. Number unlimited.

MAXIMILIAN JOSEPH, (*Bavaria.*) Founded by Maximilian Joseph, King of Bavaria, (on the elevation of that Electorate to the rank of a Kingdom,) 1806. Three Classes—Grand Crosses, (to which only General Officers are admitted,) Commanders, and Knights.

MERIT, (of *Poland.*) Founded in 1791, by Stanislaus Augustus, but soon after suppressed. Revived by Frederick Augustus Grand Duke of Warsaw, 1807. The Emperor of Russia is at present Grand Master as King of Poland.

MERIT of HOLSTEIN, or LION of LIMBOURG, is not a Royal Order: it was instituted in 1768, but soon became dormant, and remained so till 1818, when a junior Prince of the House of Saxony was named Grand Master.

MILITARY MERIT, (of *Prussia.*) Founded by Frede-
    rick the Great, 1740. One Class.

MILITARY MERIT, (of *France.*) Founded by Louis
    XV. 1759, for Protestant Officers only, they
    being excluded from the Order of St. Louis.
    Three Classes—Grand Crosses, Commanders,
    and Knights.

MILITARY MERIT, (of *Wurtemburg.*) Founded by
    Frederick II. Duke of Wurtemburg, 1799.
    Three Classes—Grand Crosses, Commanders,
    and Knights.

POLAR STAR, (*Sweden.*) Founded by Frederick I.
    1720, for civil and diplomatic services. One
    Class.

ST. ANDREW, (*Russia.*) Founded by the Emperor
    Peter I. 1698, and is the second in rank of the
    Russian Orders. One Class. Conferred only
    on Sovereign Princes, Russian Nobility of the
    first rank, or Foreigners of the highest distinc-
    tion. H. R. H. the Duke of Clarence and the
    Duke of Devonshire are the only English
    Subjects Knights of this Order. This Order
    carries with it those of St. Alexander Newski
    and St. Anne. ,

ST. ALEXANDER NEWSKI, (*Russia.*) Founded by
    the Empress Catherine, 1725, for civil as well
    as military services. One Class,

ANNE, (*Russia.*) This Order, originally founded
1735, by Charles Frederick Duke of Holstein,
is now the Fourth Order of the Russian Em-
pire. Two Classes.

BENTO D'AVIS, (*Portugal.*)   Founded by Al-
phonso King of Portugal, 1147.

CONSTANTINE, (*Naples.*)   Said to have been
founded by Constantine the Great, anno 313.
Established as a Neapolitan Order by Don Car-
los of Spain, on his Accession to the Throne of
Naples. Four Classes—Grand Crosses, Grand
Commanders, Commanders, and Knights.

ESPRIT, or HOLY GHOST, (*France.*)   Founded
by Henry III. of France, 1578, and is the
highest Order of that Monarchy.

FERDINAND and MERIT, (*Naples.*)   Founded by
the King of Naples, 1800, for the purpose of
rewarding Lord Nelson and the Officers who
served under him at the Nile, and in the reco-
very of Naples from the French Army in 1799.
Originally Two Classes — Grand Crosses, in
number, 21, and Commanders, unlimited. In
1810 a Third Class was added, the Members of
which are called Knights. The first Grand
Cross nominated was Lord Nelson, the second,
General Suvarroff, the third the Emperor
Paul I.

Sт. FERNANDO, (*Spain.*) Founded in 1811, by the Supreme Cortes, and confirmed by King Ferdinand VII. in 1815. Five Classes—the First, or Grand Crosses, for General Officers who have commanded in chief. Second, for General Officers who have particularly distinguished themselves. Third, for General Officers without distinction. Fourth, for Officers from Colonels downwards, who have particularly distinguished themselves; and the Fifth, for the same Class of Officers generally.

Sт. GEORGE, (*Russia.*) Founded by the Empress Catherine II. Four Classes. Number unlimited. To be admitted into the First Class it is necessary to have served twenty-five years, and commanded as General-in-Chief at some decisive victory; or to have made, to use the French phrase, eighteen Maritime Campaigns. The Emperor of Russia himself is not exempted from these conditions. The Emperor Paul never wore it, (though Suvarroff and others of his Generals did,) nor the late Emperor Alexander until after the Campaigns of 1812 and 1813, in which he commanded his own armies.

Sт. GEORGE and THE REUNION, (*Naples.*) Founded by Ferdinand IV. 1819.

Sт. HERMENEGILDE, (*Spain.*) Founded by King Ferdinand VII. anno 1814. Two Classes—

Grand Crosses, for General Officers; Second Class, for Officers from Brigadier downwards.

St. Januarius, (*Naples.*) Founded by Charles King of the Two Sicilies, (afterwards King of Spain,) 1738. One Class. Number limited to Sixty.

The King of Naples originally intended to confer this Order on Lord Nelson, but was prevented by the consideration that some parts of its ceremonies and statutes rendered its being held by a Protestant impossible, and therefore he founded the Order of St. Ferdinand and Merit. Subsequently, however, that difficulty was overcome, and his Grace the Duke of Wellington, and six more English Officers, now belong to it.

St. Joachim. This Order owes its foundation to no crowned head, but has been recognized both in Great Britain and abroad, as an Order of Knighthood. It was founded in 1755, and derives its chief claim to notice from having numbered Lord Nelson amongst its members.

St. John of Jerusalem. (See Malta.)

St. Joseph, (*Tuscany.*) Founded by Ferdinand III. Grand Duke of Tuscany, 1807, at Wurtzburg, of which he was then Grand Duke; and on ascending the Tuscan Throne, in 1814, he carried this Order with him and made it the second Order of Tuscany. Three Classes—

Grand Crosses, limitted to 20; Commanders, 30; Knights, unlimited. Civilians, and even Ecclesiastics, are admissible, as well as Military Men:

St. Louis, (*France.*) Founded by Louis XIV. 1695. Three Classes—Grand Crosses, Commanders, and Knights or Small Crosses.

St. Maurice and St. Lazare, (*Sardinia.*) The Order of St. Maurice was founded by Amadeus VIII. Count of Savoy, anno 1434. In 1572 that of St. Lazare (founded about 1119) was united to it. Three Classes—Grand Crosses, Commanders, and Knights.

St. Stanislaus, (*Poland.*) Founded by Stanislaus Augustus King of Poland, 1765. Renewed, and divided into Four Classes, by the Emperor Alexander, 1815.

St. Stephen, (*Tuscany.*) Founded by Cosmo de Medici, Grand Duke of Tuscany, 1561.

St. Wladimir, (*Russia.*) Instituted by the Empress Catherine II. 1782, and revived by the Emperor Alexander, 1801. This Order is Civil as well as Military, and consists of Five Classes —Grand Crosses, Commanders, Knights of the Third Class, of the Fourth Class, or Junior Knights, and the Fifth Class, which is claimable by persons who have filled a civil office for thirty-five years.

SWORD, (*Sweden.*) Instituted 1525; afterwards became dormant, and was renewed by King Frederick I. 1748. Three Classes—Grand Crosses, Commanders, and Knights.

TOWER and SWORD, (*Portugal.*) Founded by John VI. King of Portugal, 1808, on the occasion of his retreat to the Brazils, and for the purpose, as the Statutes express, of rewarding those on whom, as being " united with religious ceremonies and institutions," the Orders then existing in Portugal, could not with propriety be conferred. It consists of Three Classes—Grand Crosses, Commanders, and Knights.

WILHELM, (*Netherlands.*) Founded by the present King of the Netherlands, 1815. Four Classes —Grand Crosses, Commanders, and Knights of the Third and Fourth Classes.

ORDERS OF THE GARTER, THISTLE, BATH, ST. PATRICK, ROYAL HANOVERIAN GUELPHIC, AND ST. MICHAEL AND ST. GEORGE.

To give a List of the Knights of these Orders did not enter into the Editor's original plan, but he was induced to add them even after the first part was in the press, by the representation of some of his friends, that a Work professing to treat on subjects connected with English Knighthood, would be imperfect without them.

The Lists of the Garter and first Class of the Bath were of easy compilation, the Records of the Heralds' College furnishing complete materials. With respect to the Second Class of the Bath, and the Orders of the Thistle, St. Patrick, and Ionian, not having access to the Records of those Orders, he can only say, he has used his best industry to collect his Lists from every source within his reach, and trusts the inaccuracies in them will be few and unimportant.

For the List of the Guelphic Order he is indebted to the kindness of Dr. Kuper, Minister of the German Chapel, St. James's, Domestic Chaplain to H. R. H. the Duchess of Clarence, and Chaplain to the Hanoverian Embassy; a kindness the more marked as the Editor's first introduction to that Gentleman was for the purpose of soliciting the favour, for which he now begs to return his sincere thanks, and the more valuable as he had been previously refused the same information by the King of Arms of the Order, to whom, both as a principal functionary of the Order and a brother officer of his own, he at first applied himself.

With this single exception, the Editor has to acknowledge the most cheerful co-operation in every quarter where he has had occasion to apply for assistance or information. To his Friends, Charles George Young, Esq. York Herald, and Nicholas Harris Nicolas, Esq. he has great pleasure in expressing his particular obligations.

College of Arms,
31 May, 1828.

ADDENDA.

KNIGHTS BACHELORS.

John Macra, Esq. Lieutenant Colonel and K.C.H. Knighted 27 March, 1828.

William Ouseley, Esq. *Knighted by the Lord Lieutenant of Ireland*, Feb. 1800.

FOREIGN ORDERS.

Isaac Harte, Captain in the Army.

† Lion and Sun. 31 March, 1828.

George Read, Lieutenant R.N.

† Knt. Tower and Sword. 17 April, 1828. *Conferred by the King of Portugal when he went on board H. M. S. " Windsor Castle," in the Tagus, May*, 1824.

Sir Thomas Byam Martin, Vice Admiral of the Red. Sword of Sweden.

John Lord Macleod.

Sword of Sweden. Invested by His late Majesty, 9 Dec. 1778.

Sir Levet Hanson.

.St. Philip of Holstein.

Diploma registered in Coll. Arm. 24 Aug. 1782. St. Joachim.

P. 84, to Art. Sir William Drummond, K.C. *add* Died 29 March, 1828.

P. 160, to Art. Sir William Domett, *add* Died 19 May, 1828.

CORRIGENDA.

Page
19, Art. Sir DIGBY DENT —*for* Died about 1790 *read* Died
15 Feb. 1817.

23, Art. Sir EDWARD FELLOWES—*for* EDWARD *read* THO-
MAS. See p. 128.

33, Art. Sir JERE HOMFRAY—*read* Sir JEREMIAH HOM-
FRAY. The name, however, stands "Jere" in
the Gazette and registration of his Knighthood in
the College of Arms.

76, Art. Sir JOHN CARR—*for* Poland *read* Sicily.

90, Art. Sir JOHN GREIG—*for* JOHN *read* SAMUEL.

CONTENTS.

KNIGHTS BACHELORS.

———

ABBOTT, CHARLES, Lord Chief Justice of the King's
    Bench. 14 May, 1816. Created 30 April,
    1827, Baron Tenterden.

ADAMS, WILLIAM, (see RAWSON.)

ADDINGTON, WILLIAM, Chief Magistrate of the Po-
    lice. 1797. Died 7 April, 1811, aged 83.

AGAR, FELIX. 17 June, 1812.

AINSLIE, ROBERT. 20 Sept. 1775. Created a Baro-
    net 19 Nov. 1804. Died 22 July 1812.

AINSLIE, PHILIP, of Pilton, N. B. and Lieutenant
    Colonel of Horse Guards. 25 Feb. 1778.
    Elder Brother of the above Sir Robert A. Died
    June 1802.

AIREY, GEORGE, Major General, and K.C.H. 19
    Dec. 1820. Now Lieutenant General.

ALDERSON, GEORGE, Sheriff of London. 17 April,
    1818. Died 9 April, 1826.

ALEXANDER, JAMES, Sheriff of London. 2 March,
    1803.

B

ALEXANDER, WILLIAM, Lord Chief Baron of the Exchequer. 19 Jan. 1824.

ALGOOD, LANCELOT, of Nunwick, co. Northumberland. 3 Nov. 1760. Died about 1801.

ALTHAM, WILLIAM, Mayor of Thetford, co. Norfolk, and of Mark Hall, Essex. 13 Sept. 1786. Died 7 Aug. 1818.

ANBUREY, THOMAS, Lieutenant Colonel in the service of the East India Company, and C.B.*

ANSTRUTHER, JOHN, Chief Justice in Bengal. 4 Oct. 1797. Created a Baronet 18 May, 1798. Died 26 Jan. 1811.

ANSTRUTHER, ALEXANDER, Recorder of Bombay. 9 April, 1813, (by Patent.) Died about 1821.

ARDEN, RICHARD PEPPER, Master of the Rolls. 18 June, 1788. Appointed Chief Justice of the Common Pleas and created Baron Alvanley 1801. Died 19 March, 1804.

ARENTSCHILDT, VICTOR VON, Major in the Army and K.T.S. 20 April, 1815.

ARKWRIGHT, RICHARD, of Wirksworth, co. Derby. 22 Dec. 1796. Died 3 August, 1798.

ARUNDEL, JOHN, (then BRAZIER,) Mayor of Huntingdon. 30 May, 1800. Took the surname

---

* The Gazette announced 29 Aug. 1827, that His Majesty had been pleased to direct Letters Patent to pass the Great Seal, conferring the honour of Knighthood on this Gentleman, but the patent has not yet passed. 30 Jan. 1828.

of Arundel by Royal Sign Manual, 16 Feb. 1801.

ASHURST, WILLIAM HENRY, Judge of the King's Bench. 22 June, 1770. Retired 1798. Died at Waterstock, co. Oxford, 5 Nov. 1807, aged 82.

ASKEW, HENRY, Major General and C.B. 25 July, 1821.

ASTON, RICHARD, (late Chief Justice of the Common Pleas in Ireland,) on being appointed a Judge of the King's Bench in England. 19 April, 1765. Died 1 March, 1778.

AUCHMUTY, SAMUEL, knighted as Proxy for Sir Robert Abercrombie at the Installation of the Bath, 1803. 4 May, 1803. Nominated a Knight Companion of the Bath, and installed 1812. Died in Dublin 11 August, 1822.

AYLETT, WILLIAM, Lieutenant General and K.M.T. Never knighted, but has the rank of Knight Bachelor and appellation " Sir," having obtained His Majesty's Licence to receive the Order of Maria Theresa previous to the Regulation of 1812, relative to Foreign Orders. (*See Preface.*)

BAGHOTT, PAUL, (formerly Wathen) of Lypiatt Park, co. Glouc. 22 May, 1812. Proxy for Viscount Strangford at the Installation of the Bath, 1812. Took the surname of Baghott by Royal Sign Manual, 19 May, 1812.

BAGSHAW, WILLIAM CHAMBERS, High Sheriff of Derbyshire. 24 March, 1806. Formerly Darling—took the surname of Bagshaw 1801.

BAIRD, DAVID, Major General and K.C. 19 June, 1804, (by Patent.) Nominated a Knight Companion of the Bath, 18 August, 1804, and installed 1812. Created a Baronet 13 April, 1809.

BAKER, ROBERT, Chief Magistrate of the Police. 10 May, 1820.

BAKER, WILLIAM, Alderman of (Bassishaw Ward) London. 3 Nov. 1760. Died 23 Jan. 1770.

BALDWYN, WILLIAM BRIDGES, High Sheriff of Surrey. 1 Oct. 1762. Died about 1765.

BANNATYNE, WILLIAM M'LEOD. 21 Nov. 1763.

BANNATYNE, WILLIAM M'LEOD, late Judge of the Court of Session in Scotland. 21 Nov. 1823.

BANKES, HENRY, Alderman of (Cordwainers' Ward) London, and Sheriff of London and Middlesex, 1762. 4 Oct. 1762. Died 19 July, 1774.

BANKS, EDWARD, of Mile Town, Sheerness, co. Kent. 12 June, 1822.

BARKER, ROBERT, Major of Artillery at the Siege of

Manilla. 16 April, 1764. Afterwards Commander-in-Chief in Bengal. Created a Baronet 1781. Died 14 Aug. 1789.

BARLOW, ROBERT, Captain R.N. 16 June, 1801. Knighted for the Capture of the Africaine. French Frigate. Brother of Sir George Hilaro Barlow, K.B. who was created a Baronet 29 June, 1803. A superannuated Rear Admiral and C.B.

BARRINGTON, JONAH, D.C.L. Judge of the High Court of Admiralty in Ireland. 13 May, 1807.

BARTON, WILLIAM, Recorder of Liverpool. 9 May, 1816. Died 7 Jan. 1826.

BARTON, FREEMAN, Captain 2d Foot. 25 June, 1814.

BASSETT, RICHARD, Mayor of Newport, Isle of Wight. 29 May, 1817.

BAYLEY, DANIEL, Consul General in Russia. 20 June, 1815.

BAYLEY, FRANCIS, Recorder of Prince of Wales's Island. 21 Nov. 1823.

BAYLEY, JOHN, a Judge of the King's Bench. 11 May, 1808.

BECKWITH, THOMAS SYDNEY. 29 May, 1812. Proxy to his Brother, Sir George Beckwith, K.B. at the Installation of the Bath, 1812. Now a Major General, Colonel Commandant of the Rifle Brigade, K.C.B. and C.T.S.

BEECHY, WILLIAM, R.A. 9 May, 1798.

BELL, THOMAS, Sheriff of London. 29 April, 1816. Died 4 March, 1824.

BENNETT, WILLIAM, Sheriff of Hants. 24 Dec. 1760. Died 1815.

BERESFORD, JOHN POO, Captain R.N. 29 May, 1812. Proxy to Sir John Coape Sherbrooke, K.B. at the Installation of the Bath, 1812. Created a Baronet 21 May, 1814. Now Vice-Admiral of the Blue, K.C.B. and G.C.T.S.

BERRY, EDWARD, Captain of the Vanguard at the Battle of the Nile. 12 Dec. 1798. Created a Baronet 12 Dec. 1806. Now Rear Admiral of the White, and K.C.B.

BERTIE, THOMAS, (formerly Hoar.) 24 June, 1813. Took the surname of Bertie 1788. Died (an Admiral and Commander of the Order of the Sword of Sweden) 13 June, 1825.

BEST, WILLIAM DRAPER, Judge of the Common Pleas. 12 June, 1819. Now Chief Justice of the Common Pleas.

BETTON, JOHN, Mayor of Shrewsbury. 1816. Never gazetted.

BEWICKE, ROBERT, High Sheriff of Northumberland. 5 Dec. 1760. Died 4 Sept. 1771.

BICKERTON, RICHARD, Captain R.N. 24 June, 1773. Created a Baronet 29 May, 1778. Died 28 Feb. 1792. Father of the present Sir Richard Hussey Bickerton, Bart. K.C.

BIRNIE, RICHARD, Chief Magistrate of the Police. 17 Sept. 1821.

BISHOP, WILLIAM, Mayor of Maidstone. 4 Nov. 1778. Died 12 Jan. 1817, aged 83.

BLACKMAN, HENRY, Constable of Lewes. 29 May, 1782. Living 1827.

BLACKSTONE, WILLIAM, Judge of the King's Bench. Feb. 1770. Removed the same year to the Common Pleas. Died 14 Feb. 1780.

BLAGDEN, CHARLES. 1792. Died about 1820.

BLICKE, CHARLES, Surgeon. 16 March, 1803. Died 30 Dec. 1815.

BLIZARD, WILLIAM, 16 March, 1803. Surgeon to their R. H. the Duke and Duchess of Gloucester, a Vice President, one of the Curators of the Museum, and Honorary Professor of Anatomy and Surgery, in the College of Surgeons.

BLOOMFIELD, BENJAMIN, Major General, Clerk Marshal and Chief Equerry to H. R. H. the Prince Regent. 11 Dec. 1815. Created Baron Bloomfield, 1825. G.C.B. and G.C.H.

BLOSSETT, ROBERT HENRY, Serjeant at Law, on being appointed Chief Justice in Bengal. 19 April, 1822. Died in Calcutta 1 Feb. 1823.

BLOUNT, CHARLES BURRELL. Never knighted, but has the rank of Knight Bachelor and appellation "Sir," from having obtained His Majesty's Licence to accept the Order of Maria Theresa, previous to the Regulation of 1812, relative to Foreign Orders. (*See Preface.*)

BLOXHAM, MATTHEW, Alderman of Bridge Ward Within. 1800. Died 16 Oct. 1822, aged 79.

BOLTON, GEORGE, Preceptor to the Princesses in Writing, Geography, &c. 3 April, 1799. Died about 1807.

BOLTON, ROBERT, Major General and K.C.H. 20 Feb. 1817. Now Lieutenant General and Equerry to His Majesty.

BOLTON, WILLIAM, Captain R.N. 18 May, 1803.

BONSALL, THOMAS, High Sheriff of Cardigan. Dec. 1795. Died about 1809.

BONTEIN, JAMES. 18 July, 1798. Lieutenant Colonel, and appointed, 1816, a Gentleman of the Privy Chamber. Died in Germany, about 1820.

BOOTH, CHARLES, of Harrietsham, High Sheriff of Kent. 8 May, 1784. Died in Harley Street, 26 April, 1795.

BRANSCOMB, JAMES, Sheriff of London. 22 April, 1807. A Stock Broker and Lottery Contractor. Died at Enfield, 7 Dec. 1809, aged 74.

BRAZIER. (See ARUNDEL.)

BRETON, WILLIAM. 21 Sept. 1761. Died in Burlington Street, 8 Feb. 1773.

BRETON, LE. (See LE BRETON.)

BRIDGER, JOHN, Standard Bearer to the Band of Gentlemen Pensioners, and of Combe Place,

Sussex. 22 Sept. 1761. Died about 1817, aged 84.

BRIDGES, HENRY, High Sheriff of Surrey. 11 May, 1814.

BRYDGES, JOHN WILLIAM HEAD. 12 June, 1822. A Major in the Army, Brother to Sir Samuel Egerton Brydges, Bart.

BRISBANE, CHARLES, Captain R.N. 10 April, 1817, (by Patent.) Now Rear Admiral and K.C.B.

BRISBANE, JAMES, Captain R.N. and C.B. 23 Sept. 1815.

BROOKS, JOHN COTTERELL, High Sheriff of Herefordshire. 10 Nov. 1761. Took the surname of Cotterell. Died 29 Jan. 1790. Father of Sir John Geers Cotterell, Bart.

BROWN, CHARLES, of Margaretta Farm, co. Norfolk, M.D. and Knight of the Red Eagle of Prussia. 6 June, 1818. Sir Charles was Physician to the King of Prussia, and died 11 May, 1827, aged 80.

BROWNE, JOHN, Colonel in the Army, and K.T.S. 24 Aug. 1814, (by Patent.)

BROWNE, HENRY, Lieutenant Colonel and K.C.H. 27 July, 1826.

BRYCE, ALEXANDER, Brigadier General and Colonel of Engineers, C.B. K.C. and C.F.M. 18 Sept. 1816.

BUCHAN, JOHN, Colonel in the Army, C.B. and C.T.S. 1816. (Never gazetted.)

BUGGIN, GEORGE. 31 May, 1797. Died 12 April, 1825.

BULLER, ANTHONY, Judge in Bengal. 23 April, 1816.

BULMER, FENWICK, Senior Gentleman of the Band of Gentlemen Pensioners. 19 July, 1821. Died 8 May, 1824.

BULKELEY, JOHN. 9 Dec. 1795.

BURDON, THOMAS, of Newcastle upon Tyne. Brother-in-law of the Earl of Eldon. 14 May, 1817.

BURGMAN, GEORGE, British Commissioner under a Convention with the Emperor of Russia and King of Prussia. 10 Dec. 1813.

BURLAND, JOHN, Baron of the Exchequer. 8 April, 1774. Died 28 March, 1776.

BURNETT, ROBERT, Sheriff of London. 15 April, 1795. Died at Morden Hall, Surrey. 23 June, 1816, aged 78.

BURRELL, PETER. 6 July, 1781. Deputy Lord Great Chamberlain. Created Baron Gwydir 16 June, 1796. Died 29 June, 1820.

BURROUGH, JAMES, a Judge of the Common Pleas. 14 May, 1816.

BURROW, JAMES. 10 March, 1773. Master of the Crown Office, and sometime President of the Royal Society. Died 5 Nov. 1782, aged 81.

BURTON, JOHN, of Soho Square. 1805. Died in Soho Square, 24 Nov. 1809.

BURTON, ROBERT, a Bencher of Gray's Inn. 1800. Sometime M.P. for Wendover. Died in Charlotte Street, Fitzroy Square, 2 March, 1810.

BUSK, WADSWORTH, Attorney General of the Isle of Man. 22 June, 1781. A Bencher of the Middle Temple. Died 15 Dec. 1811.

BUTLER, EDWARD GERALD. Never knighted, but had the rank of Knight Bachelor, and the appellation "Sir," from having obtained the Royal Licence to accept the Order of Maria Theresa, before the Regulation of 1812, relative to Foreign Orders. (*See Preface.*) Died (a Major-General) about 1824 or 5.

BYAM, ASHTON WARNER, Attorney General of Grenada. 8 Oct. 1789.

BYARD, THOMAS, Captain R.N. 26 Aug. 1789. Died Oct. 1798.

CALCRAFT, GRANBY THOMAS, KM.T. and K.T.S. Never knighted, but had the rank of a Knight Bachelor, and the appellation of "Sir," from having obtained the Royal Licence to accept the Order of Maria Theresa, previous to the Regulation of 1812, relative to Foreign Orders. (*See Preface.*) Died 20 Aug. 1820.

CALDER, ROBERT, Captain R.N.   13 March, 1797.
Created a Baronet 1798.   Died (an Admiral
and K.C.B.) 31 Aug. 1818.

CAMPBELL, ALEXANDER, Lieutenant General.   29
May, 1812.   Proxy for the Duke (then Earl) of
Wellington, K.B. at the Installation of the Bath
in 1812.   Nominated a K.C.B. and created a
Baronet 6 May, 1815.   Died 11 Dec. 1824.

CAMPBELL, ARCHIBALD, Lieutenant Colonel in the
Army, and Brigadier in the Portuguese Service,
and K.T.S.   28 April, 1814.   Now Colonel
in the Army and K.C.B.

CAMPBELL, JAMES, Colonel in the Army. 9 May, 1788.

CAMPBELL, JAMES, Major General and C.B.   3 Dec.
1822.   Now K.C.B.

CAMPBELL, JOHN, Lieutenant Colonel of 4th Regiment of Portuguese Cavalry and K.T.S.   9
March, 1815.

CAMPBELL, NEIL, Colonel in the Army, and sometime
Colonel of the Corsican Rangers, C.B. K.S.A.
and K.S.G.   15 Oct. 1814.   Died (Governor
of Sierra Leone) 1827.

CARLISLE, ANTHONY, Member of the College of
Surgeons.   24 July, 1821.   Never gaz·tted.

CARR, THOMAS, of Bedingham, co. Sussex, High Sheriff of Sussex.   19 June, 1800.

CARRINGTON, CODRINGTON EDMUND, of the Middle
Temple, Barrister, D.C.L. and Chief Justice in
Ceylon.   24 June, 1801.

CARROLL, WILLIAM PARKER, Lieutenant Colonel in the Army, and a Major General in the Spanish Service. 14 May, 1816. Now a Colonel in the Army, C.B. and a Knight of Charles III.

CARTER, JOHN, Mayor of Portsmouth. 22 June, 1773. Died 17 May, 1808, aged 68.

CARTWRIGHT, JOHN, Sheriff of London. 9 Nov. 1761. Died 29 Aug. 1772.

CHALLENOR, THOMAS, Sheriff of London and Alderman of Aldgate Ward. 4 Oct. 1762. Died 8 May, 1766.

CHAMBERS, ROBERT, a Judge in Bengal. (By Patent) 14 June, 1777. Vinerian Professor of Law at Oxford, 1762. Principal of New Inn Hall, 1766. Judge in Bengal, 1773. Chief Justice there, 1791. Died near Paris, 9 May, 1803, aged 65.

CHAMBERS, CHARLES HARCOURT, Judge in Bengal. 21 Nov. 1823. A Judge in Bombay, 1827. Nephew of Sir Robert above-mentioned.

CHAMBERS, SAMUEL. 1800. Of Woodstock House, Sheriff of Kent, 1799.

CHAMBERS, WILLIAM, a celebrated Architect. Surveyor General of the Board of Works, F.R. and A.S. Never knighted, but had the rank of Knight Bachelor and appellation " Sir," from having received from the King of Sweden the Order of the Polar Star. (See Preface.) Died 8 March, 1796.

CHAMBRE, ALAN, Judge of the Common Pleas. 1800.
Resigned 1516, and died 20 Sept. 1823.

CHAPMAN, JOHN, Mayor of Windsor. 12 Nov. 1823.

CHEERE, HENRY, Deputy Lieutenant of the County of
Middlesex. 10 Dec. 1760. Created a Baronet, 18 July, 1766. Died 15 Jan. 1781.

CHESTER, ROBERT, Master of the Ceremonies to the
King. 5 June, 1818.

CHETWYND, GEORGE, of Brockton Hall, co. Stafford,
Clerk of the Privy Council. 19 Jan. 1787.
Created a Baronet 1 May, 1795. Died 24
March, 1824.

CHRISTIE, ARCHIBALD, Comm. General of Hospitals at Chatham, Colonel of the 1st Veteran
Battalion, and K.H. 28 June, 1820.

CHURCH, RICHARD, Lieutenant Colonel, C.B. and
K.C.H. Commander of Ferdinand and Merit,
and Grand Cross of the Order of St. George
and the Reunion of Naples. 12 June, 1822.

CHURCHMAN, THOMAS, Mayor of Norwich. 18
Sept. 1761. Died 4 Dec. 1781.

CLARE, MICHAEL BENIGNUS, of Spanish Town, Jamaica, M.D. 14 Sept. 1822, (by Patent.)

CLARIDGE, JOHN THOMAS, Recorder of Prince of
Wales's Island. 30 Sept. 1825.

CLERKE, JOHN, Captain R.N. 31 Jan. 1772. Died
in the East Indies, 1777.

COCHRANE, THOMAS, (commonly called Lord Cochrane.) 26 April, 1809.

COCHRANE, THOMAS JOHN, Captain R.N. 29 May, 1812. Proxy for his Father, Sir Alexander Forester Cochrane, at the Installation of the Bath, 1812.

COKE, WILLIAM, a Judge at Ceylon. 25 May, 1815. died 1819.

COLE, CHRISTOPHER, Captain R.N. 29 May, 1812. Proxy for Sir Richard Goodwyn Keats at the Installation of the Bath, 1812. Now K.C.B.

COLLIER, GEORGE, of Froyle, co. Hants, Captain R.N. 27 Jan. 1775. Died Vice (Admiral of the Blue) 6 April, 1795.

COLLIER, GEORGE RALPH, Captain R.N. 16 Sept. 1807. Created a Baronet 20 Sept. 1814. Died (K.C.B.) March, 1824.

COLLINS, JOHN, Captain R.N. 4 July, 1783. Died 1795.

COLVILLE, CHARLES HENRY. 29 May, 1812. Proxy for Sir Thomas Graham (now Lord Lynedoch) at the Installation of the Bath, 1812.

COMPTON, JOHN WOODFIELD, LL.D. late Judge of the Vice Admiralty Court at Barbadoes. 5 July, 1816. Died 1821.

COMYN, ROBERT BUCKLEY, a Judge at Calcutta. 9 Feb. 1825. At Madras, 1827.

CONANT, NATHANIEL, Chief Magistrate of the Police. 11 Nov. 1813. Died in Portland Place, 12 April, 1822, aged 77.

CONNELL, JOHN, Procurator of the Church of Scotland, and Judge of the Admiralty Court in that Kingdom. 20 April, 1826.

CONROY, JOHN, Captain in the Army, Equerry to H.R.H. the Duchess of Kent, and K.C.H. 16 Aug. 1827.

COOKE, HENRY FREDERICK, Colonel in the Army and C.B. and M.P. for Camelford. 1825. (Not gazetted.)

COOKE, WILLIAM, Judge at Ceylon. 25 May, 1815.

COOPER, GEORGE, Judge at Madras. 30 April, 1816.

COPLEY, JOHN SINGLETON, Solicitor General. Oct. 1819. Appointed Attorney General, 1824. Master of the Rolls, 1826. Lord High Chancellor, and created Baron Lyndhurst, April 1827.

CORRY, TREVOR, Consul at Dantzick. 29 March, 1776. Died about 1781.

COSBY, HENRY AUGUSTUS MONTAGU. 9 Jan. 1784. Adjutant General in India, 1773. Died (a Lieutenant General) 17 Jan. 1822.

COTGREAVE, JOHN, Mayor of Chester. 5 July, 1816.

COTTERELL, (see BROOKS.)

COTTRELL, STEPHEN, Master of the Ceremonies. 21 Dec. 1796. Died 23 May, 1818, aged 80.

COX, WILLIAM, Lieutenant Colonel in the Army, Major General in the Portuguese Service, and K.T.S. 13 Aug. 1816. Now a Colonel.

COXHEAD, THOMAS, of Epping, co. Essex. 1 Feb. 1793. Died 23 Nov. 1811, aged 77.

CRAUFURD, PHILIP, Resident for Scotch Affairs in the Netherlands. 2 May, 1777.*

CRICHTON, ARCHIBALD WILLIAM, Knight of Saint Anne 2d Class, Knight of Wladimir, and Member of the Legion of Honour. 13 March, 1817.

CRICHTON, ALEXANDER, M.D. First Physician and Counsellor of State to the Emperor of Russia, and Knight of St. Wladimir. 1 March, 1821.

CROKE, ALEXANDER, of Studley Priory, co. Oxon. LL.D. Judge of the Vice Admiralty Court, Nova Scotia. 5 July, 1816.

CUMMING, JOHN. About 1780. Colonel in the Bengal Army. Died at St. Helena, 26 Aug. 1786.

CURTIS, ROGER, Captain R.N. knighted for his services at the Siege of Gibraltar. 29 Nov. 1782. Created a Baronet 10 Sept. 1794. Died 14 Nov. 1816.

* Qu.—If his Christian name was not PATRICK? A Sir Patrick Crawfurd, Conservator of Scotch Privileges at Campvere in Holland, died 24 Jan. 1782. See Scots' Magazine, p. 110.

c

DALLAS, ROBERT, Solicitor General.   19 May, 1813.
Appointed a Judge of the Common Pleas 1813.
Chief Justice of the same Court, 1818.   Re-
tired 1823, and died 25 Dec. 1824.

DALRYMPLE, CHARLES, Commissary General to the
Army under the Duke of Wellington.   10 Nov.
1814.

DALRYMPLE, HEW WHITEFOORD, Major in the Army.
5 May, 1779.   Created a Baronet 6 May, 1815.

DALSTON, WILLIAM, High Sheriff of Cumberland.
27 Dec. 1760.

DAMPIER, HENRY, Justice of the King's Bench.   15
July, 1813.   Died 3 Feb. 1816, aged 68.

DANCE, CHARLES WEBB, Lieutenant Colonel 2d
Guards.   25 July, 1801.

DANCE, NATHANIEL, Captain in the Naval Service of
the East India Company.   11 March, 1805.
Died 25 March, 1827.

DARLING, ROBERT, Sheriff of London.   8 Oct. 1766.
Died 4 Aug. 1770.

DARWIN, FRANCIS SACHEVERELL, M.D.   10 May,
1820.

DASHWOOD, CHARLES, Captain R.N. G.C.T.S.   20
April, 1825.

DAVENPORT, THOMAS, Serjeant at Law.   27 June,
1783.   Died at York, 25 March, 1786.

DAVIDSON, DAVID, of Cautray, N. B.   22 May,
1812.

DAVIS, JOHN BREWER, Captain in the West Kent Militia. 28 Sept. 1778.

DAVISON, WILLIAM, Major in the Army, K.H. Aide-de-Camp and Equerry to H. R. H. the Duke of Cambridge. 3 Sept. 1824.

DAVY, HUMPHRY, President of the Royal Society. 9 April, 1812. Created a Baronet 20 Oct. 1818.

DAY, JOHN, Judge Advocate General in Bengal. 19 June, 1777. Died at Richmond 14 June, 1808.

DENT, DIGBY, Captain R.N. May 1778. Died about 1790.

DESANGES, FRANCIS, Sheriff of London. 17 April, 1818.

DESSE, WILLIAM, Clerk of the Cheque to the Band of Gentlemen Pensioners. 15 July, 1771. Deceased.

D'IVERNOIS, FRANCIS. 11 May, 1796.

DORMER, CLEMENT COTTRELL, Master of the Ceremonies. 15 Oct. 1779. Died 1809.

DOVETON, WILLIAM WEBBER, one of the Council at St. Helena, and Lieutenant Colonel of the Volunteers there. 3 Feb. 1819.

DOUGLAS, JAMES, Consul General at Naples. 20 April, 1765. Died at Naples, May, 1795.

DOUGLAS, ANDREW SNAPE, Captain R.N. 13 Sept. 1789. Died 4 June, 1797.

DOWNIE, JOHN, Commissary General and Brigadier General in the Portuguese Service, and Knight of Charles III. 19 May, 1813.

DOYLE, JOHN. Never knighted, but had the rank of a Knight Bachelor, and the appellation " Sir," from having obtained the Royal Licence to accept the Order of the Crescent previous to the Regulation of 1812, relative to Foreign Orders. (*See the Preface.*) Created a Baronet 29 Oct. 1805. A General, Colonel of the 87th Foot, and G.C.B.

DOYLE, JOHN MILLEY, Lieutenant Colonel, and K.T.S. 28 July, 1814.

DOYLE, CAVENDISH BENTINCK, Captain R.N. 20 April, 1825.

DRYDEN, JOHN TURNER, of Canons Ashby, co. Northampton. 15 March, 1793. Created a Baronet 2 May, 1795. Died 14 April, 1797.

DUBERLY, JAMES, of Gains Hall, Huntingdonshire. 30 March, 1803.

DUFF, JAMES, of Kinstoure, N.B. 30 April, 1779. Proxy for Sir James Harris at the Installation of the Bath, 1779.

DUMARESQ, JOHN, of Guernsey. 30 March, 1803. Died 20 March, 1819.

DUNBAR, JAMES, of Boath, N.B. Captain R.N. 30 March, 1810. Created a Baronet 19 Sept. 1814.

DUNKIN, WILLIAM, a Judge in Bengal. 18 March, 1791. Died 31 July, 1807.

DURBIN, JOHN, of Walton, co. Somerset, Mayor of Bristol. 28 Jan. 1778. Died 25 Jan. 1814, aged 80.

DURNO, JAMES, of Atrochie, N.B. Consul General at Memel. 13 March, 1799. Died at Osborne's Hotel, Adelphi, 1807.

EAMER, JOHN, Alderman of Langbourn Ward and Sheriff of London. 15 April, 1795. Lord Mayor 1801. Died 29 March, 1823, aged 74.

EARLE, JAMES, Surgeon. 1800. Died 1817.

EAST, EDWARD HYDE, Chief Justice in Bengal. 26 Feb. 1813. Created a Baronet 25 April, 1823.

ELDER, GEORGE, Colonel in the Army and K.T.S. 11 Nov. 1813.

ELIOTT, JOHN, of Peebles, M.D. 31 May, 1776. Created a Baronet 1778. Died 7 Nov. 1786.

ENGLISH, JOHN HAWKER, Knight of Gustavus Vasa, and Surgeon to the King of Sweden. 23 Feb. 1815.

ERSKINE, WILLIAM, of Torrie, co. Fife, Lieutenant Colonel. 27 July, 1763. Created a Baronet 28 July, 1791. Died (a General) April 1795.

ESDAILE, JAMES, (Alderman of Cripplegate Ward
    and) Sheriff of London. 8 Oct. 1766. Lord
    Mayor 1778. Died 6 April, 1793.

ESDAILE, JOHN, Banker. 1801.

EVANS, JOHN, of Erbistock House, High Sheriff of
    Merionethshire. 1 July, 1817. Died 1825 or
    1826.

EVANS, DAVID WILLIAM, Recorder of Bombay. 10
    May, 1820. Died 4 Dec. 1821.

EVERITT, JOHN, High Sheriff of Bedfordshire. 19
    June, 1800. Died 1 Jan. 1823, aged 64.

EYLES, JOSEPH, Captain R.N. 1795. Died 28 Nov.
    1806.

EYRE, JAMES, Baron of the Exchequer. 22 Oct.
    1772. Recorder of London 1762. Chief Ba-
    ron 1787. Lord Chief Justice of the Common
    Pleas 1793. Died 6 July, 1799.

EYRE, GEORGE, Captain R.N. 9 April, 1812. Rear
    Admiral and K.C.B. 1827.

FAIRFAX, GEORGE, Captain R.N. Captain of the
    Venerable at the Battle of Camperdown. 1797.
    Died at Edinburgh, 7 Nov. 1814, aged 76.

FARRANT, GEORGE. 19 June, 1822.

FARRINGDON, WILLIAM, High Sheriff of Lancashire.
    6 March, 1761.

FAULKENER, ARTHUR BROOKE, M.D. Physician to the Forces. 23 Feb. 1815.

FELLOWES, JAMES, M.D. 21 March, 1809. A Deputy Lieutenant of Hants 1827.

FELLOWES, EDWARD, Capt. R.N. C.B. 13 Feb. 1828.

FENOUILHET, PETER, Exon of the Yeomen of the Guard. 24 Sept. 1761. Died about 1774.

FENN, JOHN, of East Dereham, eo. Norfolk. 23 May, 1787. Died 14 Feb. 1794, aged 56.

FERGUSON, ADAM, Deputy Keeper of the Regalia in Scotland. 29 Aug. 1822.

FIELDING, JOHN, of Westminster, Police Magistrate. 30 Sept. 1761. Died 4 Sept. 1780.

FLEMING, WILLIAM, of Norwich. 5 Oct. 1761. Died about 1791.

FLETCHER, ROBERT, a Major in the East India Company's Service. 29 Dec. 1763. Died at the Mauritius, 1777.

FLETCHER, RICHARD, Lieutenant Colonel of Engineers, and Chief Engineer with the Army in the Peninsula. April, 1812. Created a Baronet 14 Dec. 1812. Killed at the Siege of St. Sebastian, 31 Aug. 1813.

FLINT, CHARLES WILLIAM. 29 May, 1812. Proxy for Sir Henry Wellesley at the Installation of the Bath, 1812. Under Secretary of State for Ireland 1827.

FLUDYER, THOMAS, of London. 29 Dec. 1761. Died 19 March, 1769. Brother of Sir Samuel

Fludyer, who was created a Baronet 1759, and Uncle of Sir Samuel Brudenell Fludyer, Bart. 1827.

FORD, RICHARD, Police Magistrate. 16 Dec. 1801. Died in Sloane Street, 3 May, 1806.

FORDYCE, WILLIAM, M.D. 16 Jan. 1783. Died 4 Dec. 1792.

FORESTI, SPIRIDION, English Resident at Corfu. 1 July, 1817.

FORREST, DIGGORY, of Plymouth. 10 May, 1815.

FOWKE, THOMAS, of Lowesby, co. Leicester. 5 May, 1779. Proxy for Sir Henry Clinton, K.B. at the Installation of the Bath, 1779. Sometime Groom of the Bedchamber to Henry Frederick Duke of Cumberland, and father of Sir Frederick Gustavus Fowke, created a Baronet 1814. Died 30 Nov. 1786.

FOWLER, JOHN D. Bailiff of Burton upon Trent. 8 Nov. 1818. Never gazetted.

FRANKLIN, WILLINGHAM, Judge at Madras. 19 April, 1822.

FRANKLIN, WILLIAM, M.D. Deputy Inspector General of Military Hospitals. 22 April, 1823.

FRANKS, JOHN, Judge at Calcutta. 20 April, 1825.

FRASER, JOHN, Lieutenant General. 27 Nov. 1826.

FREMANTLE, The Right Hon. WILLIAM HENRY, a Privy Councillor, Treasurer of the Household, and G.C.H. uncle of Sir Thomas Francis Fremantle, Bart. 31 Oct. 1827.

FULLER, JOSEPH, Lieutenant General and G.C.H. 16 Dec. 1826.

GAMBIER, JAMES, Consul General in the Nether-lands. 27 April, 1808.

GARRETT, GEORGE, of Portsmouth. 27 Sept. 1820.

GARROW, WILLIAM, Baron of the Exchequer. 17 July, 1812.

GATEHOUSE, THOMAS. 3 Sept. 1762. Died 1799.

GAZELEE, STEPHEN, Judge of the Common Pleas. 27 April, 1825.

GELL, WILLIAM. On his return from a Mission to the Ionian Islands, 14 May, 1803.

GEORGE, RUPERT. 23 May, 1803. Proxy for Sir Thomas Graves at the Installation of the Bath, 1803. Created a Baronet 18 Sept. 1809. Died 25 Jan. 1823.

GIBBES, GEORGE SMYTH, M.D. 10 May, 1820.

GIBBS, VICARY, Solicitor General. 20 Feb. 1805. Attorney General 1807. A Judge of the Com-mon Pleas 1812. Lord Chief Baron 1813. Lord Chief Justice of the Common Pleas the same year. Resigned 1818, and died 8 Feb. 1820.

GIFFORD, ROBERT, Solicitor General. 29 May, 1817. Attorney General 1819. Chief Justice of the

Common Pleas 1824.   Master of the Rolls and Deputy Speaker of the House of Lords, and created Baron Gifford, 1824.   Died 4 Sept. 1826.

GIFFARD, HARDINGE, Chief Justice of Ceylon 1819. Died 30 April, 1827.   (Not gazetted.)

GILPIN, JOSEPH, M.D.   Knighted for his services at Gibraltar and in the West Indies, 28 Feb. 1815.

GLEDSTANES, ALBERT, Lieutenant General.   Died 25 April, 1818.

GLODE, RICHARD, Sheriff of London.   24 Nov. 1790. Died at Mayfield Place, near Orpington, Kent, about Oct. 1804.

GLYNN, RICHARD CARR, Sheriff of London, and Alderman of Bishopsgate Ward.   24 Nov. 1790. Created a Baronet 1800.

GOODYERE, ROBERT, Lieutenant of the Band of Gentlemen Pensioners.   22 Sept. 1762.   Died 1 July, 1800, aged 80.

GORDON, SAMUEL, of Newark upon Trent, High Sheriff of Notts.   18 March, 1761.   Created a Baronet 21 Aug. 1764.   Died 22 April, 1780. Father of the present Sir Jenison William Gordon, Bart. 1827.

GORDON, HON. CHARLES.   29 May, 1812.   Proxy for Sir John Hope, (afterwards Earl of Hopetoun) at the Installation of the Bath, 1812. Brother of the Earl of Aberdeen.

GORDON, ALEXANDER. 19 June, 1800. Aide-de-Camp to the Duke of Wellington at the Battle of Waterloo, and mortally wounded there.

GORE, JOHN, Captain R. N. 21 Feb. 1805. Now Vice Admiral and K.C.B.

GOSLING, FRANCIS, Banker in London. 28 Oct. 1760. Died 1769.

GOTT, HENRY THOMAS, of Newlands, Bucks. 14 April, 1784. Died 14 Nov. 1809, aged 79.

GOUGH, HUGH, Colonel and C.B. 4 Dec. 1815.

GOULD, HENRY, Baron of the Exchequer. 2 Nov. 1761. Judge of the Common Pleas 1763. Died 5 March, 1794.

GOULD, CHARLES, Judge Advocate General. 5 May, 1779. Created a Baronet 1792. Died Dec. 1806. Father of the present Sir Charles Morgan Gould, 1827.

GOWER, ERASMUS, Captain R.N. 1 Aug. 1792. Died (Admiral of the White) at the Hermitage, Hambledon, 21 June, 1814, aged 72.

GRAHAM, ROBERT. 19 June, 1800.

GRAHAM, ROBERT, Baron of the Exchequer. 1822. Retired in Feb. 1827.

GRANT, The Right Hon. WILLIAM, D.C.L. Master of the Rolls. 1799. Resigned 1817.

GRANT, JAMES ROBERT, M.D. Inspector General of Hospitals, and Chief of the Medical Staff of the Army under the Duke of Wellington in the Netherlands and France. 18 March, 1819.

GRANT, JOHN PETER, a Judge at Bombay. 30 June, 1827.

GRANT, WILLIAM KEIR (formerly KEIR.) Never knighted, but has the rank of Knight Bachelor and appellation of " Sir," from having obtained the Royal Licence to accept the Order of Maria Theresa previous to the Regulation of 1812, respecting Foreign Orders. (*See Preface.*)

GREEN, CHARLES, Major General. 4 May, 1803. Created a Baronet 5 Dec. 1805. Now a General and Colonel 37th Foot.

GREY, WILLIAM DE, Justice of the Common Pleas. 28 Jan. 1771. Created Baron Walsingham 1780. Died 9 May, 1781. Grandfather of the present Baron Walsingham.

GREY, CHARLES EDWARD, Judge at Madras. 17 May, 1820. Chief Justice at Calcutta 1827.

GREY, THOMAS, M.D. 30 Nov. 1819.

GROSE, NASH, Judge of the King's Bench. 9 Feb. 1787. Retired 1813. Died 31 May, 1814, aged 74.

GUNSTON, THOMAS, High Sheriff of Somersetshire. Oct. 1762.

GWILLIM, HENRY, Judge at Madras. 16 July, 1801.

HALL, ROBERT, Captain R.N. C.B. and K.C.F.M. 15 July, 1816. Died Commissioner of the Navy in Canada, 7 Feb. 1818, aged 39.

HALLIDAY, ANDREW, M.D. 26 Jan. 1821. Physician to H. R. H. the Duke of Clarence, and K.H.

HALLIFAX, THOMAS, Alderman of Aldersgate Ward, London. 5 Feb. 1778. Sheriff 1769, and Lord Mayor 1777-8. Died 7 Feb. 1789.

HAMILTON, ALEXANDER, Sheriff of Devon. 18 Aug. 1786. Died at Retreat, near Exeter, 12 June, 1809.

HAMILTON, WILLIAM OSBORNE, Lieutenant Colonel, and late Governor of Heligoland. 25 May, 1815. Died at Manor House, Windsor, 5 June, 1818, aged 68.

HAMILTON, EDWARD, Captain R.N. 3 Feb. 1800. Created a Baronet 1818. Now Rear Admiral and K.C.B.

HAMILTON, JOHN, Lieutenant General. 15 July, 1813. Created a Baronet 1815. G.C.T.S.

HAMMOND, ANDREW SNAPE. 1778. Created a Baronet 18 Dec. 1783.

HAMMETT, BENJAMIN, Alderman of Portsoken Ward, London. 11 Aug. 1786. Died 22 July, 1800.

HANKEY, RICHARD. 18 May, 1803. Proxy for Sir Andrew Mitchell at the Installation of the Bath, 1803. Deceased.

HANKIN, THOMAS PATE, Lieutenant Colonel. 22
    Aug. 1822. Died 26 Oct. 1825.

HARRINGTON, EDWARD, Mayor of Bath. 27 May,
    1795.

HARRIS, THOMAS, Sheriff of London. 28 Aug. 1765.
    Died at Finchley, 15 June, 1782.

HART, ANTHONY, Vice Chancellor of England. 30
    April, 1827.

HART, WILLIAM, Sheriff of London. 16 Oct. 1760.
    Died 22 Aug. 1765.

HART, WILLIAM. (Never knighted, but enjoyed the
    rank of Knight Bachelor, and the appellation
    " Sir," from having received the Order of Sta-
    nislaus from the King of Poland.)

HARTWELL, FRANCIS JOHN. 4 May, 1803. Proxy
    for Lord Keith at the Installation of the Bath,
    1803. Created a Baronet 1805.

HARWOOD, BUSIC, Professor of Anatomy at Cam-
    bridge. 11 June, 1806. Died, Vice Master
    of Downing College, 10 Nov. 1814.

HARVEY, LUDFORD. 19 May, 1813. Late Ex-
    aminer of the College of Surgeons.

HARVEY, ROBERT JOHN, Lieutenant Colonel and
    K.T.S. 6 Feb. 1817.

HARVEY, JOHN, Lieutenant Colonel, K.C.H. and C.B.
    15 Dec. 1824.

HAVILAND, DE, PETER, Bailiff of Guernsey. 6
    March, 1817.

HAWKINS, JOHN, Chairman of the Middlesex Ses-
sions. 23 Oct. 1772. Died 21 May, 1789.

HAWKS, ROBERT SHAFTO, of Gateshead, co. Durham.
21 April, 1817.

HAY, GEORGE, D.C.L. Principal of the Court of
Arches, and Judge of the Admiralty. 11 Nov.
1773. Died 6 Oct. 1778.

HAYWARD, THOMAS, of Carswell, Berks, Clerk of
the Cheque to the Band of Gentlemen Pensioners. May, 1799. Died 2 Nov. 1799.

HEARD, ISAAC, Garter King of Arms. 2 June, 1786.
Died 29 April, 1822.

HEATHCOTE, JOHN EDENSOR, High Sheriff of Stafford. 8 March, 1784.

HEATHCOTE, HENRY, Captain R.N. About 1820.
Now Rear Adm. of the Blue. (Not gazetted.)

HELLIER, SAMUEL, High Sheriff of Worcester. 17
Sept. 1762. Died 12 Oct. 1784.

HENSLOW, JOHN, Surveyor of the Navy. 20 March,
1793. Died at Sittingbourne, 21 Sept. 1815,
aged 86.

HEREFORD, JAMES, High Sheriff of Hereford. 22
Dec. 1760. Died 1786.

HERNE, WILLIAM, Alderman of Castle Baynard
Ward. 14 Jan. 1797. Died about 1800-1.

HERRIES, ROBERT, a Banker and Colonel of the City
Light Horse Volunteers. 25 Feb. 1774. Died
at Cheltenham, 25 Feb. 1815, aged 85.

HERRIES, WILLIAM LEWIS, Lieutenant Colonel, Quarter Master General in the Mediterranean, K.C.H. and Register and Secretary of the Most Honourable Military Order of the Bath. 29 May, 1826.   Now one of the Comptrollers of Army Accounts.

HERRIOTT, FREDERICK GEORGE, C.B.   16 March, 1822.

HETLEY, RICHARD, of Alwalton, co. Huntingdon, Sheriff of Cambridge and Huntingdon.   11 June, 1800.   Died 20 Jan. 1807, aged 69.

HILL, ROBERT CHAMBRE, Proxy for his Brother, Sir Rowland Hill (now Lord Hill) at the Installation of the Bath, 1812.   29 May, 1812.   Colonel in the Army.

HILL, THOMAS NOEL, Lieutenant Colonel, K.T.S. 28 July, 1814.   Now K.C.B.

HILL, DUDLEY ST. LEGER, Colonel and K.T.S.   25 Nov. 1816.

HILLMAN, WILLIAM, Mayor of Winchester.   18 Aug. 1786.   Clerk of the Board of Green Cloth.   Died in St. James's Palace, 7 Feb. 1793.

HITCHINS, EDWARD, Mayor of Oxford.   June, 1812. Died at Oxford, 21 Nov. 1825.

HODGSON, RICHARD, Mayor of Carlisle.   30 Dec. 1795.

HOLROYD, GEORGE SOWLEY, Judge of K. B.   14 May, 1816.

HOMFRAY, JERE, of Llandaff House, co. Montgomery.
22 Nov. 1809.

HOLLOWAY, CHARLES, Major of Engineers. 2 Feb.
1803. Died a Major General 1826.

HOOD, ALEXANDER. 22 May, 1812. Proxy for his
Uncle, Sir Samuel Hood, at the Installation of
the Bath 1812. Succeeded his Uncle as Baronet 1814.

HOPE, JOHN, Lieutenant General, G.C.H. 30 March,
1821.

HOPKINS, JOHN, Lord Mayor of London. 12 Oct.
1792. Alderman of Castle Baynard Ward
1782. Died at Snaresbrook 14 Oct. 1796.

HOTHAM, RICHARD, of Merton, co. Surrey. 12
April, 1769. M.P for Southwark, and founder
of Hothampton, or Bognor, Sussex. Died 13
March, 1799, at a very advanced age.

HOTHAM, BEAUMONT, Baron of the Exchequer. 17
May, 1775. Succeeded as Lord Hotham 1813.
Died 4 March, 1815.

HUDDART, JOSEPH-BRYNKER, of Brynker, co. Car-
marthen. 8 Aug. 1821.

HUGHES, EDWARD, Capt. R. N. 27 Oct. 1773.
Nominated K.B. 1778. Installed 1779. Died,
Vice Admiral of the Blue, 17 Jan. 1794.

HUGHES, WILLIAM BULKELEY. 4 May, 1803.

HULLOCK, JOHN, Baron of the Exchequer. 21 April,
1812.

D

HULSE, SAMUEL. A General, and G.C.H. Treasurer
of the Household. 1821. (Not gazetted.)

HUNTER, JOHN, Consul General in Spain. 10 Dec.
1813. Died at Bordeaux 3 July, 1816.

HUTCHINSON, WILLIAM, Major General. 6 May,
1820. Now Lieutenant General.

JAY, Dr. JAMES, of New York. 25 March, 1763.

JAMIESON, JOHN, M.D. Knight of G. Vasa. 19
May, 1813.

JARDINE, HENRY, King's Remembrancer of the Exchequer in Scotland. 20 April, 1825.

JELF, JAMES, Alderman of Gloucester. 28 July,
1814.

JEYNES, EDWIN. 1799. (Gazetted 19 June, 1800.)
Banker at Gloucester. Died 1 Oct. 1810.

IMPEY, ELIJAH, Chief Justice in Bengal. 30 March,
1774. Died 1 Oct. 1809.

JODRELL, PAUL, M.D. 26 Oct. 1787. Physician
to the Nabob of Arcott. Died at Madras
1803.

JOHNSON, JOHN. 22 Nov. 1765. Succeeded his
father, Sir William Johnson, Bart. 1774.

JOHNSTON, ALEXANDER, Chief Justice in Ceylon.
1 Nov. 1809.

JONES, THOMAS, of Stanley, co. Salop, High Sheriff
of Shropshire. 23 Dec. 1760. Died about
Feb. 1782, aged 49.

JONES, OWEN, a Gentleman Pensioner. 22 Sept.
1761. Died 6 Nov. 1766.

JONES, WILLIAM, Judge at Calcutta. 19 March,
1783. Died in Bengal 1794.

KEIR. (See GRANT.)

KEITH, BASIL, Capt. R. N. 10 June, 1772. Proxy
for his brother, Sir Robert Murray Keith, at
the Installation of the Bath 1772. Governor
of Jamaica 1773 to 1777. Died 1777.

KEITH, ALEXANDER, Knight Marshal of Scotland.
20 July, 1819.

KELLEY, GEORGE, of Bishopsdown, co. Kent, and
Sheriff of that County. 29 Sept. 1762. Died
14 Nov. 1771.

KENT, THOMAS, High Sheriff of Surrey. 16 Oct.
1771. Died 6 Jan. 1802, aged 83.

KERRISON, ROGER, of Norwich, Banker. 1800.
Died 13 June, 1808.

KERRISON, EDWARD, C.B. 5 Jan. 1815. (Not gazetted.) Created a Baronet 1821. A Major
General and K.C.H.

KER, CHARLES, of Gateshaw, co. Roxburgh, M.D. 19 April, 1822.

KEMEYS, ROBERT JONES ALLARD, Lieutenant Colonel, of Ynisarwed, co. Glamorgan, Esq.   6 March, 1817.

KENNEDY, ROBERT HUGH, Commissary General. 8 May, 1812.

KITE, ROBERT, Sheriff of London.   16 Oct. 1760. Alderman of Lime Street Ward.   Died 2 Sept. 1772.

KING, RICHARD, Captain R. N.   5 June, 1784. Created a Baronet 1792.   Died in Nov. 1806.

LACON, EDMUND, of Great Yarmouth.   19 Dec. 1792.   Created a Baronet 1818.   Died 3 Oct. 1820.

LANGSTONE, STEPHEN, Alderman of Bread Street Ward, and Sheriff of London.   26 Oct. 1796. Died 5 Nov. 1797.

LAWRENCE, THOMAS, President of the Royal Academy.   20 April, 1815.   A Member of the Legion of Honour.

LAWRENCE, SOULDEN, Judge of King's Bench.   12 March, 1794.   Judge of Common Pleas 1808. Died 8 July, 1814.

LAW, EDWARD, Attorney General. 20 Feb. 1800. Appointed Chief Justice of the King's Bench and created Baron Ellenborough 1802. Died 13 Dec. 1818.

LAURENT, PETER FRANCIS, of Grenada, (then recently ceded by France, and the first native of the ceded Islands on whom the honour was conferred.) 22 Feb. 1768.

LAURIE, PETER, Sheriff of London. 7 April, 1824.

LEACH, JOHN, Vice Chancellor of England. Jan. 1817. Appointed Master of the Rolls 1827.

LE BRETON, THOMAS, Bailiff of Jersey. 20 April, 1825.

LE BLANC, SIMON, Judge of the King's Bench. 1798. Died 15 April, 1815.

LEIGHTON, WILLIAM, Alderman of Billingsgate Ward, London. 21 May, 1800. Died 22 April, 1826.

LESTER, JOHN, of Poole, co. Dorset. 2 June, 1802. Died at Bath, 12 Jan. 1805.

LEVER, ASHTON, of Alkrington, co. Lancaster. 1778. Died 24 Jan. 1788.

LEWES, WATKIN, Alderman of Lime Street Ward, London. 5 Feb. 1773. Alderman of Bridge Ward Without 1804. Sheriff 1772, Lord Mayor 1780-1. Died 13 July, 1821.

LILLIE, JOHN SCOTT, Major in the Army. 6 March, 1816.

LINDSAY, JOHN, Captain R. N. 10 Feb. 1764. Nominated K.B. 1771. Died 1788.

LITTLE, JAMES, of Teneriffe. (By Patent.) 22 Nov. 1816.

LITTLEDALE, JOSEPH, Judge of the King's Bench. 9 June, 1824.

LIND, JAMES, Captain R. N. 9 May, 1805. K.C.B. 1815. Died about 1823.

LOCK, JOSEPH, Mayor of Oxford. 13 June, 1814.

LONG, WILLIAM, Mayor of Bedford. 28 July, 1814.

LOWE, HUDSON, Colonel of the Corsican Rangers. 26 April, 1814. Now Major General and K.C.B.

LUMSDEN, HENRY NIVEN. 5 July, 1816. Created a Baronet 1820. Died 1822.

MACARTNEY, GEORGE, Ambassador at St. Petersburgh. 19 Oct. 1764. Installed K.B. 1772. Created Earl Macartney in Ireland and Baron Macartney in Great Britain. Died 31 March, 1806.

MACARTHY, CHARLES LYRAGH, Colonel in the Army and Governor of Sierra Leone. 22 Nov. 1820. Killed at Cape Coast Castle, Africa, 24 Jan. 1824.

MACDONALD, ARCHIBALD, Solicitor General. 27 June, 1788. Chief Baron of the Exchequer 1793. Created a Baronet 1813. Died 18 May, 1826.

MACKENZIE, ALEX. 10 Feb. 1802. Died 1820.

MACKINTOSH, JAMES. 21 Dec. 1803. Professor of General Polity and the Laws in the East India College.

MACLEAN, LAUCHLAN, M.D. Alderman of Sudbury. 18 July, 1812.

M'CLEOD, ALEXANDER, C.B. Lieutenant Colonel E.I.C.S. 29 Aug. 1827. (By Patent.)

MACNAUGHTEN, FRANCIS, Judge at Madras. 1 Nov. 1809.

Mc GRIGOR, JAMES, M.D. Inspector of Hospitals. 28 July, 1814.

MADDEN, GEORGE ALLEN, Major General, C.B. and K.T.S. 5 July, 1816.

MALCOLM, JOHN, Lieutenant Colonel E.I.C.S. and Ambassador to Persia. 15 Dec. 1812. Now G.C.B. and K.L S.

MANN, HORATIO. 10 June, 1772. Proxy for his uncle, Sir Horatio Mann, at the Installation of the Bath 1772. Succeeded his uncle as a Baronet 1786. Died 2 April, 1814.

MANSFIELD, JAMES, Chief Justice of the Common Pleas. May, 1804. Solicitor General 18 Nov. 1783. Died 23 Nov. 1821, aged 88.

MANTELL, THOMAS, Mayor of Dover.   10 May, 1820.

MARRIOTT, JAMES, LL.D.   1778.   Judge of the Admiralty Court, Master of Trinity Hall, Cambridge, and sometime M.P. for Sudbury.   Died at Turnstead Hall, Suffolk, 21 March, 1803.

MARSH, CHARLES, of Reading, Berks.   23 Aug. 1786.   Died about 1804.

MATTHIAS, HENRY, High Sheriff of Pembroke.   29 May, 1816.

MAXWELL, MURRAY, Captain R. N.   28 May, 1818. C.B.

MEADE, JOHN, M.D. Deputy Inspector of Hospitals. 5 Nov. 1816.

MENDS, ROBERT, Captain R. N. Knight of Charles III.   27 May, 1815.   Died, Commander of His Majesty's Squadron on the Coast of Africa, 1824.

MEREDYTH, JOHN, High Sheriff of Brecon.   8 Sept. 1762.

MILES, JONATHAN, Sheriff of London.   22 April, 1807.   Died 22 July, 1821, aged 60.

MILES, EDWARD, Lieutenant Colonel, C.B. and K.T.S.   27 Nov. 1826.

MILLS, THOMAS, Town Major of Quebec.   5 June, 1772.   Proxy for Sir Ralph Payne, (afterwards Lord Lavington) at the Installation of the Bath 1772.   Died about 1806.

MITCHELL, CHARLES, Captain E.I.C.S. 18 March, 1796. Knighted for an action in the Straits of Molucca, with a French frigate, he being then Captain of the *William Pitt*, East Indiaman.

MITFORD, JOHN, Solicitor General. 15 Feb. 1793. Attorney General 1801. Appointed Lord High Chancellor of Ireland and created Baron Redesdale, 1802.

MOLYNEUX, FRANCIS, Gentleman Usher of the Black Rod. 18 Sept. 1765. Died 9 June, 1812.

MONK, JAMES, late Chief Justice in Canada. 27 April, 1825. Died at Cheltenham 18 Nov. 1826, aged 82.

MONTRESOR, HENRY TUCKER, Lieutenant General. 17 April, 1818. K.C.B. and G.C.H.

MOORE, GEORGE, Speaker of the House of Keys in the Isle of Man. 22 June, 1781.

MORTLOCK, JOHN CHETHAM, Mayor of Cambridge. 5 July, 1816.

MOUBRAY, ROBERT, of Cockernay, co. Fife, Lieutenant Colonel in the Army. 20 April, 1825.

MUNDAY, THOMAS, Mayor of Oxford. 24 Sept. 1761. Died 27 Oct. 1772.

MUNRO, GEORGE, of Poyntzfield, co. Cromarty. 30 April, 1779. Proxy for Sir Hector Munro at the Installation of the Bath 1779. Died 1785.

MUNRO, ALEXANDER, Consul at Madrid. 17 March, 1783.

NAGLE, EDMUND, Captain R. N. 1795. Now Vice Admiral, K.C.B. and G.C.H.

NAPIER, JAMES, Superintendant of Hospitals in Jamaica. 13 March, 1778. Died 21 Dec. 1799, æt. 98.

NARES, GEORGE, Judge of Common Pleas. 27 Jan. 1771. Died 20 July, 1786, in his 70th year.

NASH, NATHANIEL, Sheriff of London. 9 Nov. 1761. Died 28 August, 1769.

NASH, STEPHEN, Sheriff of Bristol. 18 Aug. 1786. Died about 1796.

NAYLER, GEORGE, York Herald, Genealogist of the Bath, and Blanc Coursier Herald. 25 Nov. 1813. Now Garter Principal King of Arms, C.T.S. and K.H.

NEVILLE, GARRETT, Sheriff of Dublin. 22 March, 1820.

NEWBOLT, JOHN HENRY, of Portswood House, Hants, Chief Justice at Madras. 17 April, 1810. Died 22 Jan. 1823, aged 53.

NICHOLL, JOHN, LL.D. King's Advocate General. 31 Oct. 1798. Now a Privy Councillor, Dean of the Peculiars, Principal of the Court of Arches, and Master of the Prerogative Court of Canterbury.

NIXON, ECCLES, Major General. 3 Dec. 1799. Died about 1806.

NORTON, FLETCHER, Solicitor General. 25 Jan. 1762. Attorney General 1763. Chief-Justice in Eyre 1769. Speaker of the House of Commons 1780. Created Baron Grantley 1782. Died 1 Jan. 1789.

NOURSE, CHARLES, of Oxford, Surgeon. 15 Aug. 1786. Died 19 April, 1789, æt. 75.

NOWELL, MICHAEL, Sheriff of Cornwall. 25 Aug. 1786. Died about 1802.

OGLE, CHALONER, Captain R. N. High Sheriff of Hants. 22 Nov. 1768. Created a Baronet 1816. Died Admiral R. N. Aug. 28, 1816, in his 89th year.

OMMANEY, FRANCIS MOLYNEUX. 17 May, 1820. Of Norfolk Street, London, Navy Agent, and late M.P. for Barnstaple.

ORMSBY, CHARLES MONTAGU. 21 May, 1806. Created a Baronet 1812. Died 3 March, 1818.

OSBORNE, SIR GEORGE, of Chicksands, Bedfordshire. 5 June, 1772, on being appointed Proxy for H. R. H. Frederick Duke of York, at the approaching Installation of the Bath.   Died 29 June, 1818.

OTTLEY, RICHARD, Judge at Ceylon. . 22 March, 1820. Now Chief Justice there.

OTWAY, LOFTUS WILLIAM, Major General, C.B.   15 Jan. 1815. (Not gazetted.)

OWEN, ARTHUR DAVIES, of Glansevern, co. Montgomery. 28 July, 1814. Adjutant General in East Indies, and Colonel in the Army. Died 18 Oct. 1816.

PAGE, THOMAS HYDE, Lieutenant Engineers.   22 Aug. 1783. Died at Boulogne June 30, 1821.

PAGET, Hon. CHARLES, Captain R.N.   1822. (Not gazetted.) Now Rear Admiral and K.C.H.

PALMER, RALPH, Judge at Madras. 24 Nov. 1824. Now Chief Justice there.

PARK, JAMES ALLAN, Judge of Common Pleas.   14 May, 1816.

PARKER, PETER, Captain R.N.   10 June, 1772. Proxy for Sir John Moore, Bart. at the Installation of the Bath 1772. Created a Baronet 1782. Died 21 Dec. 1811.

PARKER, HYDE, Captain R. N. 21 April, 1779. Died an Admiral 16 March, 1807.

PATEY, JAMES, High Sheriff of Berks. 23 Feb. 1784. Of Reading. Died 1787.

PAUL, ONESIPHORUS, High Sheriff of Gloucester. 17 Dec. 1760. Created a Baronet 1762. Died 21 Sept. 1774.

PAXTON, WILLIAM. 16 March, 1803. Died 10 Feb. 1824, aged 80.

PEACOCK, WARREN MARMADUKE. 27 July, 1815. Major General, K.C. and K.T.S.

PEAKE, HENRY, Surveyor of the Navy. 25 June, 1814. Died 1822 or 3.

PEARSON, RICHARD. 19 April, 1780. Died Lieutenant Governor of Greenwich Hospital, 25 Jan. 1805.

PEATE, ROBERT, (in Holy Orders, Rector of Brentford.) Never knighted, but has the rank of Knight Bachelor and the appellation "Sir," from having obtained His Majesty's Licence to accept the Order of St. Stanislaus of Poland previous to the Regulation of 1812, relative to Foreign Orders. (*See the Preface.*)

PEGGE, CHRISTOPHER, M.D. 26 June, 1799. Regius Professor of Physic at Oxford. Died 3 Aug. 1822.

PELLEW, EDWARD. Created a Baronet 1796; Baron Exmouth 1814; Viscount Exmouth 1816; and G.C.B.

PENNINGTON, ISAAC, Regius Professor of Medicine in the University of Cambridge. 2 Dec. 1795. Died 3 Feb. 1817, aged 72.

PERRYN, RICHARD, Baron of the Exchequer. 3 April, 1776. Died 2 Jan. 1803, in his 81st year.

PHILLIPS, JONATHAN, of Launceston. 13 April, 1786. Sometime M.P. for Camelford. Died 6 Sept. 1798.

PHILLIPS, CHARLES, Major General. 6 March, 1817.

PHILLIPS, RICHARD, Sheriff of London. 30 March, 1808.

PICKNELL, GEORGE, Mayor of Arundel. 22 April, 1795. Died about 1809.

PIGOTT, ARTHUR, Attorney General. 12 April, 1806. Died 6 Sept. 1819.

PINHORN, JOHN, of Ningwood, Isle of Wight. 19 May, 1802.

PIOZZI, JOHN SALUSBURY. 21 April, 1817. (See SALUSBURY.)

PITCHES, ABRAHAM, High Sheriff of Surrey. 12 April, 1782. Died 10 April, 1792, in the 60th year of his age.

PLESTOW, THOMAS BERNERS. About 1818. (Not gazetted.) Died 1819.

PLOMER, WILLIAM, Alderman of London. 12 April, 1782. Sheriff 1774. Lord Mayor 1781. Died 20 Aug. 1801.

PLOMER, WILLIAM, Alderman of London. 1 Nov. 1809. Sheriff 1810. Died April 12, 1812.

PLUMER, THOMAS, Solicitor General. 15 April, 1807. Attorney General 1812. Judge of the Common Pleas 1813. Master of the Rolls 1818. Died 24 March, 1824.

POCOCK, ISAAC, of Maidenhead Bridge, Berks, Sheriff of Northamptonshire. 6 Sept. 1786. Died 8 Oct. 1810.

POCOCK, GEORGE BARTHOLOMEW, Standard Bearer of the Band of Gentlemen Pensioners. 19 July, 1821.

PORTEN, STANIER, Under Secretary of State. 5 June, 1772. Proxy for Sir George Macartney at the Installation of the Bath 1772.

PORTER, JAMES, Minister at Brussels. 21 Sept. 1763. Afterwards Ambassador at Constantinople. Died 9 Dec. 1776.

PORTER, ROBERT KERR. 2 April, 1813.

POWELL, ALEXANDER, Deputy Recorder of Salisbury. 25 Aug. 1762. Died April 1, 1784.

POWELL, GABRIEL, High Sheriff of Carmarthenshire. 2 July, 1800. Died in May, 1814.

POWELL, GEORGE, Secretary of Lower Canada. 6 April, 1796.

POCKLINGTON, ROBERT. Never knighted, but has the rank of Knight Bachelor, and the appellation "Sir," from having obtained His Majesty's

Licence to receive the Order of Maria Theresa previous to the Regulation of 1812, relative to Foreign Orders. (*See the Preface.*)

PRATT, CHARLES, Chief Justice of the Common Pleas. Dec. 1761. Attorney General 1759. Baron Camden 1765. Earl Camden 1786. Died 18 April, 1794. aged 30.

PROTHERO, HENRY. 16 March, 1803.

PRITZLER, THEOPHILUS, Major General and C.B. 3 Dec. 1822. Now Lieutenant General and K.C.B.

PRYCE, CHARLES, High Sheriff of Oxford. 4 March, 1761. Died in 1803.

PULTENEY, SIR JAMES MURRAY, Bart. 18 May, 1803. Proxy for Sir William Medows at the Installation of the Bath 1803. General in the Army, Colonel of the 18th Foot. Died April 26, 1811.

PULLER, CHRISTOPHER, Chief Justice in Bengal. 28 Oct. 1823. Died at Calcutta, in May, 1824.

PYE, THOMAS, Admiral of the Blue. 24 June, 1773. Died Admiral of the White, about 1788.

PYNN, HENRY, Colonel in the Army. 23 Feb. 1815. K.T.S.

QUERINI, TOMASO, Venetian Ambassador. 28 April, 1768.

QUENTIN, GEORGE AUGUSTUS, Colonel in the Army. 8 Dec. 1821. Now C.B. and K.C.H.

RAEBURN, HENRY, President of the Academy, and First Portrait Painter to the King in Scotland. 29 Aug. 1822. Died 6 July, 1823.

RAFFLES, THOMAS STAMFORD, Lieutenant Governor of Java. 29 May, 1817. Died 5 July, 1826.

RAWLINS, WILLIAM, Sheriff of London. 13 May, 1802.

RAWLINSON, THOMAS, Alderman of London. 28 Oct. 1760. Died 3 Dec. 1769.

RAWLINSON, WALTER, Alderman of London. 4 March, 1774. Died 13 March, 1805.

RAWSON, WILLIAM, (late ADAMS, an Oculist). 1814. Died 4 Feb. 1827.

READE, THOMAS, Lieutenant Colonel, Deputy Adjutant General at St. Helena. 27 Nov. 1815.

REYNETT, JAMES HENRY, Lieutenant Colonel. 4 Dec. 1823. K.C.H. Military Secretary and Equerry to H. R. H. the Duke of Cambridge.

REYNOLDS, JOSHUA, President of the Royal Academy, F.R. and A.S. LL.D. 21 April, 1769. Died 23 Feb. 1792.

E

REW, SKEARS, of Coventry. 3 Nov. 1815.

RICE, RALPH, Recorder of Prince of Wales's Island. 29 May, 1817. Afterwards a Judge in Bombay and Bengal.

RICHARDSON, JOHN, Judge of Common Pleas. 3 June, 1819.

RICHARDS, RICHARD, Baron of the Exchequer. 11 May, 1814. Appointed Chief Baron 1816. Died 11 Nov. 1823.

RICKETTS, GEORGE WILLIAM, Judge at Madras. 23 March, 1825.

ROBINSON, SEPTIMUS, Gentleman Usher of the Black Rod. 10 April, 1761. Died 5 Sept. 1765.

ROBINSON, THOMAS, Bart. 23 Sept. 1761. (Represented the Duke of Normandy at the Coronation of King George III.) Died 3 March, 1777.

ROBINSON, CHRISTOPHER, LL.D. King's Advocate General. 5 Feb. 1809. Judge of the Consistory Court.

ROBINSON, WILLIAM HENRY, Commissary General in Canada. 2 July, 1817.

ROCHE, PHILIP KEATING. 14 May, 1816. C.B. K.C.H. and Knight of Charles III.

ROMILLY, SAMUEL, Solicitor General. 12 Feb. 1806. Died Nov. 2, 1818.

ROOKE, GILES, Judge of Common Pleas. 13 Nov. 1793. Died 1808.

ROSE, JOHN WILLIAM, Recorder of London. 24 Nov. 1790. Died 11 Oct. 1803.

ROYDS, JOHN, Judge at Bengal. 15 July, 1801. Died there 24 Sept. 1817.

RULE, WILLIAM, Surveyor of the Navy. 27 June, 1794. Died 3 Dec. 1815.

RUMFORD, COUNT. (See THOMPSON.)

RUSSELL, HENRY, Judge in Bengal. 10 May, 1797. Afterwards Chief Justice. Created a Baronet 1812. One of His Majesty's Most Honourable Privy Council. .

RUSH, WILLIAM BEAUMARIS. 19 June, 1800.

RYAN, EDWARD MICHAEL. Never knighted, but had the rank of Knight Bachelor and the appellation "Sir," from having obtained his Majesty's Licence to accept the Order of Maria Theresa previous to the Regulation of 1812, relative to Foreign Orders. (*See the Preface.*) Died March 1812.

RYCROFT, HENRY, Knight Harbinger. 4 Jan. 1816. Not gazetted.

RYAN, EDWARD, Judge at Calcutta. 27 Nov. 1826.

ST. JOHN, HENRY. 24 Dec. 1760. .

SALUSBURY, JOHN SALUSBURY PIOZZI. 21 March, 1817.

SANDERSON, JAMES, Alderman of London. 6 Oct. 1786. Created a Baronet 1795. Sheriff 1798. Lord Mayor 1792. Died at Wandsworth 21 June, 1798.

SANDYS, WINDSOR EDWARD BAYNTUN, eldest Son of Sir Edwin Bayntun Sandys, Bart. 11 April, 1825.

SAUMAREZ, JAMES, Captain R.N. 6 Nov. 1793. Nominated K.B. 1801. Created a Baronet 1801.

SAUMAREZ, THOMAS, Major in the Army. 15 July, 1795. Now Lieutenant General.

SCARLETT, JAMES, Attorney General. 30 April, 1827.

SCOTT, JOHN, Solicitor General. 27 June, 1788. Appointed Attorney General 1793. Lord Chief Justice of the Common Pleas, and created Baron Eldon 1799. Lord High Chancellor 1801 to 1806, and 1807 to 1827. Created Earl of Eldon 7 July, 1821.

SCOTT, WILLIAM, King's Advocate General. 24 Sept. 1788. Appointed Judge of the High Court of Admiralty 1798, and created Baron Stowell 17 July, 1821.

SEARLE, FRANCIS, of Kingston, co. Surrey. 30 March, 1803.

SENHOUSE, JOSEPH, Mayor of Carlisle. 7 April, 1783.

SEPPINGS, ROBERT, Commissioner of the Navy. Knighted on board the Royal George Yacht, under sail and the Royal Standard flying. 17 Aug. 1819. (Not gazetted.)

SEVESTRE, THOMAS. Never knighted, but had the rank of Knight Bachelor and the appellation "Sir," from having obtained his Majesty's Licence to accept the Order of the Tower and Sword previous to the Regulation of 1812, relative to Foreign Orders. (*See the Preface.*)

SEWELL, THOMAS, Master of the Rolls. 30 Nov. 1764. Died 6 March, 1784.

SEWELL, JOHN, LL.D. 25 May, 1815.

SEYER, WILLIAM. 1798.

SHADWELL, Right Hon. LANCELOT, Vice Chancellor of England. 16 Nov. 1827.

SHAFTO, CUTHBERT. 9 Dec. 1795.

SHAIRP, STEPHEN, Consul General in Russia. 17 Sept. 1806. Died in Edinburgh about Nov. 1826.

SHARP, CUTHBERT, Mayor of Hartlepool. 28 July, 1814.

SHEPHERD, SAMUEL, Solicitor General. 11 May, 1814. Attorney General 1816. Now Chief Baron in Scotland.

SHIPLEY, CHARLES, of the Engineers. 11 March, 1808. Major General in the Army and Colonel of Engineers. Governor of Grenada.

Died at Grenada, Nov. 30, 1815, in his 59th
year.

SILVESTER, BAPTIST JOHN, Physician to the Army
in the Low Countries, M.D. F.R.S. 21 July,
1774. Physician to the London Hospital.
Died 2 Nov. 1789.

SIMPSON, EDWARD, LL.D. Dean of the Arches, and
Judge of the Prerogative Court of Doctors'
Commons. M.P. for Dover. Dec. 1761.
Died 20 May, 1764.

SKYNNER, JOHN, Chief Baron. 23 Nov. 1777.
Died at Bath 26 Nov. 1805, aged 82 years.

SLADE, THOMAS, Surveyor of the Navy. 27 Jan.
1768. Died 24 Feb. 1771.

SMITH, WILLIAM SIDNEY. Never knighted, but had
the rank of a Knight Bachelor and the appel-
lation " Sir," from having obtained the Royal
Permission to accept the Order of the Sword of
Sweden previous to the Regulation of 1812,
relative to Foreign Orders. (*See the Preface.*)
Now Admiral of the White, K.C.B. K.C. K.S.
K.T.S. &c.

SMITH, GEORGE, Colonel in the Army, and Aide de
Camp to the King. 9 Dec. 1807. Died 1809.

SMITH, JAMES EDWARD, M.D. of Norwich, President
of the Linnean Society. 28 July, 1814. Died
17 March, 1828.

SMITH, CHARLES FELIX, Lieut. Col. Royal Engineers, and Knt. of Charles III. 10 Nov. 1814.

SMITH, LIONEL, Major General and C.B. 3 Dec. 1822.

SPICER, SAMUEL, of Portsea, Hants. 6 March, 1817. Died about 1823.

STAINES, WILLIAM, Sheriff of London. 26 Oct. 1796. Alderman 1793. Sheriff 1797. Lord Mayor 1801. Died at Clapham 11 Sept. 1807.

STAINES, THOMAS, Captain R.N. 6 Dec. 1809. K.C.B. and C.F.M.

STANDIDGE, SAMUEL, sometime Mayor of Hull. 18 Nov. 1795. Died 11 Feb. 1801, aged 75.

STANLEY, EDMOND, Chief Justice at Madras. 11 March, 1807.

STEELE, ROBERT, Lieutenant of Marines, Lieutenant Colonel in Spanish Service, and Knight of Charles III. 26 Feb. 1817.

STIRLING, WALTER, Captain R.N. 23 March, 1781. Died 24 Nov. 1786. His son, Sir Walter, was created a Baronet 1800.

STODDART, JOHN, LL.D. President of the High Court of Appeal and Judge of the Vice-Admiralty Court at Malta. 27 July, 1826.

STRANGE, ROBERT, (an eminent engraver.) 5 Jan. 1787. Died 5 July, 1792, at his house in Great Queen Street, Lincoln's Inn Fields.

STRANGE, THOMAS ANDREW, sometime Chief Justice at Madras. 14 March, 1798.

STRUTH, WILLIAM JOHN, of Redland, co. Gloucester, and of the city of Bristol. 20 April, 1815.

STUART, JOHN, Major General. 20 June, 1804. Nominated K.B. 1806. Installed 1812. Died 1815.

SULLIVAN, BENJAMIN, a Judge at Madras. 17 July, 1801. Died 1810. Elder brother of Sir Richard Sullivan, Bart.

SUTTON, CHARLES, Lieutenant Colonel, and Colonel of the 9th Portuguese Infantry. Now Colonel and K.C.B. 13 July, 1814.

SUTTON, THOMAS MANNERS, Solicitor General. 19 May, 1802. Appointed a Baron of the Exchequer 1805. Lord Chancellor of Ireland, and created Baron Manners 1807.

SWEEDLAND, CHRISTOPHER, of Lambeth. 11 Dec. 1812.

TAUNTON, WILLIAM ELIAS, Town Clerk of Oxford. 13 June, 1814. Died 3 Aug. 1825.

TAWNEY, RICHARD, Senior Alderman of Oxford. 13 Aug. 1786. Died at Oxford 5 Oct. 1791, in his 71st year.

TAYLOR, ROBERT, Sheriff of London. 25 Jan. 1783. Architect to the Bank of England. Died 27 Sept. 1788.

TEBBS, BENJAMIN, Sheriff of London. 12 Oct. 1792. Died 31 Dec. 1796, in Leicester Square.

THOMAS, NOAH, M.D. Physician in Ordinary to the King. 15 March, 1775. Died at Bath 17 May, 1792.

THOMPSON, ALEXANDER, Baron of the Exchequer. 7 Feb. 1787. Died at Bath, April 15, 1817, in his 73d year.

THOMPSON, BENJAMIN, Colonel of His Majesty's Regiment of American Dragoons. 23 Feb. 1784. Created Count Rumford by the Elector of Bavaria, and Knight of the White Eagle and St. Stanislaus of Poland. Died 1814.

THOMPSON, HENRY CLEMENTS. Never knighted, but had the rank of Knight Bachelor and the appellation " Sir," from having obtained his Majesty's Licence to receive the Order of the Sword of Sweden previous to the Regulation of 1812, relative to Foreign Orders. (*See the Preface.*)

THOMPSON, THOMAS BOULDEN, Captain R.N. 13 Feb. 1799. Created a Baronet 1806. Nominated G.C.B. 1822. Died Vice Admiral of the Red, 3 March, 1828.

THOROWGOOD, THOMAS, High Sheriff of Suffolk 1760. 9 Feb. 1761. Died at Kersey, co. Suffolk, 18 Dec. 1794.

THOROTON, Rev. JOHN. 4 Jan. 1814. Died about 1820.

TINDAL, NICOLAS CONYNGHAM. 27. Nov. 1826. Solicitor General.

TOBIN, JOHN, Mayor of Liverpool. 10 May, 1820.

TOLLER, SAMUEL, Advocate General at Madras. 9
April, 1812. Died 19 Nov. 1821.

TOMLINS, THOMAS EDLYNE, Barrister. 29 June,
1814. Now Bencher of Inner Temple.

TOWNLEY, CHARLES, Clarenceux King of Arms. 22
Sept. 1761. Afterwards Garter King of Arms.
Died at Islington 8 June, 1774.

TRAFFORD, CLEMENT, High Sheriff of Lincolnshire.
11 Nov. 1760. Died 1 Jan. 1786.

TRANT, NICHOLAS. Never knighted, but had the
rank of Knight Bachelor and the appellation
" Sir," from having obtained his Majesty's
Licence to accept the Order of the Tower
and Sword previous to the Regulation of
1812, relative to Foreign Orders. (See the
Preface.)

TRAVERS, ROBERT, Major General and C.F.M.

TREACHER, JOHN. Feb. 1786.

TREISE, CHRISTOPHER, High Sheriff of Cornwall.
23 Feb. 1761. Died 4 Dec. 1780.

TROLLOPE, HENRY, Captain R.N.   Oct. 1797,
K.C.B. and Admiral.

TRUMAN, BENJAMIN, High Sheriff of Herts. 16
Jan. 1761. Died 20 March, 1780.

TRÜTER, JOHANNES ANDREAS, late Senior Justice at
the Cape of Good Hope. (By Patent.) 11
Dec. 1823.

TURNER, BARNARD, Sheriff of London. 16 Jan. 1784. Died 15 June, 1784, in his 48th year.

TURNER, JOHN CRICHLOE, High Sheriff of Cambridge. 13 Feb. 1786. Died about 1815.

TURNER, THOMKINS HILGROVE, Lieutenant General, Lieutenant Governor of Jersey, and Groom of the Bedchamber. 28 July, 1814.

TUTHILL, GEORGE LEMAN, M.D. 28 April, 1820.

TYLDEN, JOHN MAXWELL, Major. 22 May, 1812. Proxy for Sir Samuel Auchmuty at the Installation of the Bath 1812.

TYRWHITT, THOMAS, Gentleman Usher of the Black Rod. 8 May, 1812.

VANHATTEN, JOHN, of Dinton, co. Bucks. 21 Jan. 1760.

VAVASOUR, PHILIP, High Sheriff of Cambridge. 21 Jan. 1760. Died at Wisbech 1796, aged 76.

VAUGHAN, RICHARD, of Bristol and of Redland Court, co. Gloucester. 20 April, 1815.

VERNON, EDWARD, Captain R.N. Knighted on board the *Barfleur*, the King's Standard then flying. 24 June, 1773. Died Vice Admiral of the White 1794.

VON ARENTSCHILDT, VICTOR, Lieutenant Colonel Portuguese Artillery and K.T.S.   20 April, 1815.

URMSTON, JAMES BRABAZON, President of Supercargoes at Canton in China, (by Patent.) 28 April, 1824.

WALDO, TIMOTHY, of Clapham, co. Surrey.   12 April, 1769.   Died at Clapham Jan. 10, 1786.

WALKER, PATRICK, Gentleman Usher of the White Rod, and Hereditary Usher of Scotland.   28 July, 1814.

WALLACE, JAMES, Captain R.N.   12 Feb. 1777. Died Admiral of the Blue, about 1803.

WARD, THOMAS, High Sheriff of Northamptonshire. · 16 Nov. 1761.   Died 5 Oct. 1778.

WATHEN, SAMUEL, High Sheriff of Gloucestershire. 16 March, 1803.

WATSON, WILLIAM, M.D. and Trustee of the British Museum. 6 Oct. 1786.   Died 10 May, 1787.

WATSON, JAMES, Serjeant at Law.   10 June, 1795. Died about 1800.

WATSON, WILLIAM. 18 March, 1796. Died about 1825.

WATSON, HENRY, Lieutenant Colonel, K.T.S. (by Patent.) 18 Jan. 1817.

WATSON, FREDERICK BEILBY, Master of the Household. 16 May, 1827.

WAY, GREGORY HOLMAN BROMLEY, Lieutenant Colonel. K.T.S. 28 July, 1814.

WEBB, JOHN, Director General of the Ordnance Medical Department, Woolwich. 23 Feb. 1821.

WELCH, RICHARD, Sheriff of London. 2 March, 1793. Died at Eltham 19 Dec. 1809.

WEST, EDWARD, Recorder of Bombay. 5 July, 1822. Now Chief Justice at Calcutta.

WEST, AUGUSTUS, M.D. Deputy Inspector of Hospitals and Physician in Ordinary to the King of Portugal, C.T.S. 24 Nov. 1824.

WESTPHALL, GEORGE AUGUSTUS, Captain R.N. 7 April, 1824.

WETHERELL, CHARLES, Solicitor General. 10 March, 1824. Attorney General 1826, and again 1828.

WHALLEY, SAMUEL ST. SWITHIN BURDEN, of Furze-brook House, co. Devon. 23 May, 1827.

WHITE, HENRY, Mayor of Portsmouth. 25 June, 1814. Died at Bath 1823, æt. 61.

WHITCOMBE, SAMUEL, of Thornton House, Greenwich, Kent. 14 Dec. 1812. Died 4 June, 1816.

WHITTINGHAM, SAMUEL FORD, Lieutenant Colonel, C.B. and K.C.H. 3 May, 1815.

WHITWORTH, CHARLES, M.P. for Minehead, and Lieutenant Governor of Tilbury Fort. 19 Aug. 1768. Died 22 Aug. 1778.

WHITWORTH, FRANCIS, Lieutenant Colonel Royal Artillery. 18 May, 1803. Died 26 Jan. 1805, æt. 49.

WIGRAM, ROBERT, eldest son of Sir Robert Wigram, Bart. 7 May, 1818.

WILLOCK, HENRY, Major E.I.C.S. and K.L.S. 30 June, 1827.

WILLOUGHBY, NISBET, Captain R.N. C.B. 30 June, 1827.

WILSON, HENRY, Captain 1st Life Guards. 23 July, 1794. Took the name of Wright before that of Wilson, 1814.

WILSON, THOMAS, High Sheriff of Kent. 21 Jan. 1760. Died 3 Jan. 1775.

WILSON, JOHN, Judge of Common Pleas. 15 Nov. 1786. Died 18 Oct. 1792.

WILSON, JOHN, Brigadier General in the Portuguese Service, K.T.S. 11 May, 1814. Now Major General.

WILSON, GIFFIN, Recorder of Windsor. 18 Nov. 1823. Appointed a Master in Chancery 1826.

WILSON, ROBERT. Never knighted, but has the rank of Knight Bachelor and the appellation " Sir," from having obtained His Majesty's Licence to accept the Order of Maria Theresa previous to the Regulation of 1812, relative to Foreign Orders. (*See the Preface.*)

WILLIAMS, JOHN, Surveyor of the Navy. 27 Sept. 1771. Died about 1786.

WILLIAMS, THOMAS, Captain R.N. June 1796. Now Vice Admiral of the Red and K.C.B.

WILLIAMS, DANIEL. June 1802. Chief Magistrate of Lambeth Street Police Office.

WILLIAMS, JAMES, of Kentish Town. 7 April, 1824.

WILLIAMS, JAMES, an English officer in the Austrian Service, and Commander of the Flotillas of Gun Vessels on the Danube and the Italian Lakes in 1796 and 1799. Never knighted, but had the rank of Knight Bachelor and appellation "Sir," as a Knight of Maria Theresa.

WILDER, FRANCIS JOHN, Lieutenant General, and sometime M.P. for Arundel. 29 May, 1817. Died 23 Jan. 1824.

WILLES, FRANCIS, sometime Under Secretary of State. 11 Aug. 1784. Died 30 Oct. 1827, aged 92.

WITHERS, CHARLES SCRIBSHAW, of Worcester. 6 Aug. 1788. Died at Dripshill 24 Sept. 1804.

WINTRINGHAM, CLIFTON, M.D. Physician Extraordinary to His Majesty. 14 Feb. 1762. After-

ward Physician in Ordinary and Physician General to the Army.   Created a Baronet 7 Nov.
1774.   Died 10 Jan. 1794, aged 84.

WOOD, GEORGE, Major General E.I.C.S.   1807.
K.C.B. 1815.   Died 1 March, 1824.

WOOD, JAMES ATHOLL, Captain R.N.   1 Nov. 1809.
Now Rear Admiral of the White and C.B.

WOOD, GEORGE ADAM, Major General.   22 May,
1812.   Proxy to Sir J. C. Sherbrooke, K.B.
1812.   K.C.H.

WOOD, GABRIEL, Commissary General.   20 April,
1825.

WOOD, ALEXANDER, Knight Commander of the
Ionian Order.   About 1821.

WRIGHT, JAMES, Minister of Venice.   3 July, 1766.
Died about 1786.

WRIGHT, SAMSON, Chief Magistrate at Bow Street.
1783.   Died 31 March, 1793.

WYLIE, JAMES, M.D. Councillor of State and First
Physician to the Emperor of Russia, and K.W.
At Ascot Races 1814.   (Not gazetted.)   Cre-
ated a Baronet 2 July, 1814.

WYNNE, WILLIAM, LL.D. Principal of the Court of
Arches and Master of the Prerogative Court.
24 Sept. 1788.   Afterwards a Lord of Trade,
and Master of Trinity Hall, Cambridge.   Died
11 Dec. 1815, aged 87.

WYNN, WILLIAM, Captain in the Army and Captain
of Sandown Fort.   2 May, 1810.

WYLDE, JOHN, LL.D. Chief Justice at the Cape of Good Hope. 30 June, 1827.

XIMENES, MORRIS, of Bear Place, Berks, High Sheriff of that County. 16 April, 1806.

YATES, JOSEPH, Judge of the King's Bench. 16 Dec. 1763. Judge of the Common Pleas, 1769. Died 7 June, 1769.

YEO, LUCAS, Captain R.N. and Knight of St. Bento D'Avis. 20 June, 1810. Died on the Coast of Africa, 1818.

YORKE, JOSEPH SYDNEY, Captain R.N. 21 April, 1805. Now Vice Admiral of the Red and K.C.B.

YOUNGE, GEORGE, Captain R.N. 24 Aug. 1781. Died Admiral of the White, 1816.

F

KNIGHTS OF FOREIGN ORDERS.

N.B. The dates in this List immediately following the Names of the several Orders, are those of the Royal Licences authorising the acceptance thereof.

† signifies that such Licence has been duly recorded in the College of Arms.

Where no date is annexed, no Royal Licence has been granted.

𝔓.𝔖. signifies that the Order or Orders to which it refers were conferred for general services during the Peninsular War.

𝔚. signifies that the Order or Orders it refers to were among those placed by the Allied Sovereigns at the disposal of the Duke of Wellington after the Battle of Waterloo, and by him distributed among the British officers.

Other services are printed in italics immediately after the Orders to which they refer.

ABERCROMBY, Hon. ALEXANDER, Colonel in the Army.

    † Kt. Tower and Sword. 7 Oct. 1814. 𝔓.𝔖.
    Maria Theresa.   } 𝔚.
    St. George, 4th Class. }

ACLAM, GEORGE, Captain R.N.

    † St. Anne, 2d Class. 12 Feb. 1814.
    Siege of Dantzick, 1813-14.

A'COURT, CHARLES ASHE, Lieutenant Colonel in the Army and K H. sometime Adjutant General of H. M. Forces in Italy.

    † Comm. Ferdinand and Merit.

    † Kt. of St. Maurice and St. Lazare.   } 5 March, 1816.

    Repulse of the French Troops from Sicily, and Siege of Genoa.

ACTON, Sir JOHN, Bart. many years Prime Minister to the King of Naples. Died 12 Aug. 1811.

    St. Januarius.

    St. Stephen of Tuscany.

ADAM, Sir FREDERICK, Major General, K.C.B.

    St. Anne, 1st Class.   } 𝔚𝔄.

    Maria Theresa.

AIREY, Lieutenant General Sir GEORGE, K.C.H. Knighted 1820.

    † St. Joseph.   24 Sept. 1819.

    Defence of Porto Ferrajo, 1801.

ALTEN, Major General CHARLES Count, G.C.B. G.C.H.   23 March, 1816.

    † Comm. Tower and Sword.   𝔓.𝔖.

    St. Anne, 1st Class.   } 𝔚𝔄.

    Wilhelm, 3d Class.

ANDERSON, ALEXANDER, Lieutenant Colonel, C.B.

    † Kt. Tower and Sword.   28 Nov. 1816.

    𝔓.𝔖.

ANGLESEA, Marquess of.

      Comm. Maria Theresa. ⎱
      St. George, 2d Class. ⎰ ℨℨ.

ANSON, Sir GEORGE, Major General and K.C.B.

      † Comm. Tower and Sword. 11 May, 1813.
      ℬ.ℬ.

ARBUTHNOT, Right Hon. CHARLES, Ambassador to
    the Ottoman Porte.

      † Crescent. 5 March, 1801.

ARBUTHNOT, Colonel Sir ROBERT, K.C.B.

      † Comm. Tower and Sword. 12 March,
      1813. ℬ.ℬ.

ARENTSCHILDT, FREDERICK.

      Wilhelm, 4th Class. ⎱
      St. Anne, 2d Class. ⎰ ℨℨ.

ARENTSCHILDT, Sir VICTOR, Major, C.B. and K.H.

      † Kt. Tower and Sword. 7 April, 1815. ℬ.ℬ.

ARMSTRONG, FREDERICK, Captain in the Army and
    Major in the Portuguese Service.

      † Kt. Tower and Sword. 1 March, 1820.
      ℬ.ℬ.

ARMSTRONG, RICHARD, Lieutenant Colonel in the
    Portuguese Service, C.B.

      † Kt. Tower and Sword. 14 Dec. 1816.
      ℬ.ℬ.

ASHWORTH, CHARLES, Colonel and C.B.

      † Comm. Tower and Sword. 14 Nov. 1814.
      ℬ.ℬ.

AUBIN, THOMAS, Captain in the Army.

 Knight of St. Joseph.   3 Nov. 1818.

 Aid de Camp to Lord Burghersh in the Neapolitan Campaign.

AUSTIN, JOHN, Lieutenant Colonel, Brigadier General in the Portuguese Service.

 † Comm. Tower and Sword.   18 Oct. 1821.

 𝔇.𝔖.

AYLETT, WILLIAM, Major General.

 † Maria Theresa.   30 May, 1801.

 Rescue of the Emperor Francis from the French Cavalry in Flanders, 24 April, 1794.

AYLMER, Hon. FREDERIC WILLIAM, Captain R.N. C.B.

 † Comm. of St. Ferdinand and Merit.   7 March, 1817.

 Battle of Algiers.

BAIRD, Sir DAVID, General, G.C.B. and Bart.

 † Crescent.   31 Dec. 1803.

 Campaign in Egypt, 1801.

BAKER, THOMAS, Rear Admiral and C.B.

 † Wilhelm, 3d Class.   16 Feb. 1818.

 Disembarking a body of seamen on the Coast of Holland, Nov. 1813.

BALL, ALEXANDER JOHN, Captain R.N. Created a
Baronet 1801.   Died 20 Oct. 1809.

    † Comm. St. Ferdinand and Merit.   7 Jan.
    1801.

    Re-conquest of Naples from the French 1799.

BANKS, FRANCIS, Captain R.N.

    † St. Anne, 2d Class. } 11 Nov. 1814.
    † Sword of Sweden.

    Blockade of the Elbe, Operations before Ham-
    burgh, and Siege of Gluckstadt, 1813.

BARING, GEORGE, Lieutenant Colonel, K.C.H.

    Wilhelm, 4 Class. ⚔.

BARNARD, Sir ANDREW, K.C.B. and K.C.H.

    Maria Theresa. } ⚔.
    St. George, 4th Class.

BARNES, Sir EDWARD, Major General, K.C.B.

    Maria Theresa. } ⚔.
    St. Anne, 1st Class.

BARNS, JAMES STEVENSON, Major General, C.B.

    † Kt. Tower and Sword.   27 July, 1815.
    ⚑.

BARRY, DAVID, M.D. Surgeon to the Forces, and
late First Surgeon of the Portuguese Army.

    † Kt. Tower and Sword.   26 Sept. 1825.

    Services in the field while in the actual service
    of the King of Portugal.

BECKWITH, CHARLES, Lieutenant Colonel, C.B.

    † St. Anne, 1st Class.   3 March, 1822. ⚔.

BECKWITH, Sir THOMAS SYDNEY, Major General and K.C.B.

　† Comm. Tower and Sword.　11 March, 1813.　𝔇.𝔖.

BENTHAM, GEORGE, Captain R.N.

　† Kt. of St. Maurice and St. Lazare.　25 June, 1817.

　Battle of Algiers.

BENTHAM, SAMUEL, Colonel in the Russian Army.

　† St. George of Russia.　16 July, 1789.

BERESFORD, Sir JOHN POO, Bart. K.C.B.

　† Grand Cross of the Tower and Sword.　12 Sept. 1821.

BERESFORD, WILLIAM CARR, Viscount Beresford.

　† Conde di Trancoso in Portugal, and Grand Cross of the Tower and Sword. } 18 Oct. 1811.

　† Grand Cross of St. Fernando.　24 July, 1815.

　† Grand Cross of St. Hermenegilde.　27 March, 1817.

　Grand Cross Charles III.

　Grand Cross Ferdinand and Merit.

BERKELEY, Sir GEORGE HENRY FREDERICK, Lieutenant Colonel and Assistant Adjutant General. K.C.B.　Now Colonel.

　† Kt. of the Tower and Sword.　28 Jan. 1814.　𝔇.𝔖.

　Wladimir, 4th Class. } 𝔲𝔲.
　Wilhelm, 4th Class. }

BERTIE, Sir THOMAS, Kt. Rear Admiral.   Died 13
June, 1825.
  † Comm. of the Sword of Sweden.   15 May,
  1813. 𝔇𝔖.
BETHUNE, HENRY LINDSAY, of Kilconquhar.
Lion and Sun.
BICKERTON, Sir RICHARD HUSSEY, Bart. Admiral of
the White.
  † Crescent.   25 Oct. 1804.
BINGHAM, Sir GEORGE RIDOUT, Major General and
K.C.B.
  † Comm. Tower and Sword.   30 March,
  1813. 𝔇𝔖.
BLAKENEY, Sir EDWARD, Major General, K.C.B.
  † Kt. Tower and Sword.   6 April, 1813.
  𝔇𝔖.
BLOUNT, CHARLES BURRELL.
  † Maria Theresa.   30 May, 1801.
  *Rescue of the Emperor Francis from the
  French Cavalry in Flanders, 24 April,* 1794.
BLUNT, RICHARD, Major General.
  † Comm. Tower and Sword.   7 Feb. 1815.
  𝔇𝔖.
BOURGEOIS, PETER FRANCIS, R.A.
  † Merit of Poland.   12 April, 1791.
BRACE, EDWARD, Captain R.N. and C.B.
  † Charles III.   28 Feb. 1822.
  Defence of Cadiz, 1811.

† Wilhelm, 3d Class.   28 Feb. 1822.
Battle of Algiers.

† St. Maurice and St. Lazare.   24 May, 1824.
Capture of Genoa and Battle of Algiers.

BRACKENBURY, EDWARD, Major.

    † Kt. Tower and Sword.   7 Dec. 1824.   𝔓.𝔖.

BRADFORD, Sir HENRY HOLLIS, K.C.B.   Died near
    Brussels, 17 Dec. 1816.

    Wladimir, 4th Class.   } 𝔚𝔞.
    Wilhelm, 4th Class.

BRADFORD, THOMAS, Major General, K.C.B.

    † Comm. Tower and Sword.   14 Nov. 1814.
    𝔓.𝔖.

BROKE, Sir CHARLES.   (See VERE.)

BROWN, Sir CHARLES, of Margaretta Farm, co. Nor-
    folk, M.D.   Died 11 May, 1827, æt. 80.

    † Red Eagle of Prussia, 3d Class.   23 May,
    1817.
    *Services as First Physician to the King of
    Prussia, his Court and Army.*

BROWNE, Sir JOHN, Lieutenant Colonel in the Army.

    † Kt. Tower and Sword.   } 𝔓.𝔖.
       25 Jan. 1813.

    Kt. Charles III.

BRYCE, Sir ALEXANDER, Colonel of Engineers.   C.B.

    † Comm. of St. Ferdinand and Merit.   24
    Aug. 1814.
    Defence of Sicily.

BUCHAN, Sir JOHN, Colonel, C.B.

          † Comm. Tower and Sword. 4 April, 1816.
          𝔓.𝔖.

BULL, ROBERT, Lieutenant Colonel of Artillery.

        St. Anne, 2d Class. 𝔘𝔖.

BURGH, Sir ULYSSES. (Vide DOWNES, Lord.)

BURGHERSH, JOHN Lord, G.C.H. C.B.

          † Knight of Maria Theresa. 9 June, 1814.

        Campaign of 1813.

          † Grand Cross of St. Ferdinand and Merit.
          27 July, 1815.

        Services in the Operations leading to the Re-
        storation of the King of Naples.

          † Grand Cross of St. Joseph. 3 November,
          1818.

        Neapolitan Campaign.

BURGOYNE, JOHN FOX, Lieutenant Colonel, C.B.

          † Kt. Tower and Sword. 24 May, 1815.
          𝔓.𝔖.

BUTLER, Major General Sir EDWARD GERALD.

        Died about 1824—5.

          † Kt. Maria Theresa. 30 May, 1801.

        Rescue of the Emperor Francis from the
        French Cavalry, 24 April, 1794.

BYNG, Sir JOHN, Lieutenant General and K.C.B.

        Wladimir, 4th Class. } 𝔘𝔖.
        Maria Theresa.

CADOGAN, Hon. GEORGE, Captain R.N.

† Kt. Maria Theresa. 13 July, 1814.

Services with the Austrian Army in the Adriatic, 1813.

CALCRAFT, Sir GRANBY THOMAS. Died 20 Aug. 1820.

† Kt. of Maria Theresa. 30 May, 1801.

Rescue of the Emperor Francis from the French Cavalry, 24 April, 1794.

† Kt. Tower and Sword. 9 April, 1814. 𝔓.𝔖.

CAMAC, BURGESS, Lieutenant Colonel 1st Life Guards.

† Charles III. 3 Aug. 1815, 𝔓.𝔖.

CAMERON, JOHN, Lieutenant Colonel 92d Foot.

† Kt. Tower and Sword. 15 May, 1815. 𝔓.𝔖.

CAMERON, ALEXANDER, Lieutenant Colonel.

St. Anne, 2d Class. 𝔚.

CAMPBELL, Sir ARCHIBALD, Major General and K.C.B.

† Comm. Tower and Sword. 20 Oct. 1813. 𝔓.𝔖.

CAMPBELL, Sir COLIN, Major General and K.C.B.

† Kt. of Maria Theresa.
† St. George, 4th Class.
† Maximilian Joseph.
† Comm. Tower and Sword.
28 March, 1816.
} 𝔓.𝔖. *and Battle of Waterloo.*

CAMPBELL, Sir JAMES, Major General, K.C.B.

    † Kt. Tower and Sword.   11 March, 1816.
    𝔓.𝔖.

CAMPBELL, Sir JAMES, of Inverneil, Bart. Lieutenant
    General, G.C.H. Died 1819.

    † Comm. of St. Ferdinand and Merit. 27
    June, 1816.

    Repulse of the French Attack on Messina, 18
    Sept. 1810, *and* 𝔓.𝔖.

CAMPBELL, Sir JOHN, Lieutenant Colonel, K.C.B.

    † Kt. Tower and Sword.
    14 June, 1815.
               } 𝔓.𝔖.
    † Comm. Tower and Sword.
    5 Oct. 1825.

CAMPBELL, Sir NEIL, Kt. Lieutenant Colonel and
    C.B. Died in Sierra Leone, 1827.

    St. Anne, 2d Class. } 2 June, 1814.
    St. George, 2d Class.

    Services with the Allied Armies, 1813.

CAMPBELL, WILLIAM, Lieutenant Colonel.

    St. Anne, 2d Class. 𝔚𝔩.

CAMPBELL, PATRICK, Major of Artillery.

    † Charles III. 23 July, 1816. 𝔓.𝔖.

CARR, Sir WILLIAM HENRY, Lieutenant Colonel,
    K.C.B. Died 18 Aug. 1821.

    † Kt. Tower and Sword. 15 May, 1815.
    𝔓.𝔖.

CARR, Sir JOHN.

    † St. Constantine of Poland. 8 Sept. 1810.

CARROL, CHARLES MORGAN.

Kt. Charles III. 20 May, 1816.

Defence of the Breach at Tariffa with a Company of the 87th Foot, 31 Dec. 1811.

CARROL, Sir WILLIAM PARKER, Kt. Colonel and C.B. Charles III. 20 May, 1816. } *P.S. and Battle of Tamames.*

CATHCART, WILLIAM Earl, Ambassador Extraordinary to Russia, 1813.

† St. Andrew.
† St. George, 4th Class. } 6 May, 1814.

Services with the Russian Army, 1813.

CATHCART, Hon. FREDERICK.

† St. Anne, 2d Class. 2 June, 1814.

Services with the Russian Army, 1813.

CATHCART, Hon. GEORGE.

† Wladimir, 4th Class. 3 June, 1814.

Services with the Russian Army, 1813.

CAVAN, RICHARD Earl of.

† Crescent. 19 April, 1803.

CHAMBERS, WILLIAM. Died 1796.

Polar Star of Sweden.

CHURCH, Sir RICHARD, Kt. C.B. and K.C.H. Lieutenant Colonel.

Comm. Ferdinand and Merit.
Grand Cross of St. George } 4 Oct. 1820.
and Reunion of Naples.

Military operations which led to the King's restoration to the throne of Naples.

CLANCARTY, Earl of.
> Marquess of Heusden in the Netherlands.

CLARENCE, H. R. H. WILLIAM HENRY Duke of, &c.
> St. Esprit.
> . St. Andrew.
> Black Eagle of Prussia.

CLARKE, JOHN.
> Charles III.   14 April, 1815.   𝔇.𝔖.

CLARKE, WILLIAM COLIN, Captain in the Army.
> Small Cross Ferdinand & Merit.   4 Feb. 1819.
> *Siege of Genoa,* 1814.

CLARKE, ISAAC BLAKE, Lieutenant Colonel.
> St. Anne, 2d Class.   𝔘𝔘.

CLIFTON, ARTHUR BENJAMIN, Colonel and C.B.
> St. Anne, 2d Class.   } 𝔘𝔘.
> Wilhelm, 4th Class.   }

CLINTON, Sir HENRY, Lieutenant General and G.C.B.
> Maria Theresa.
> St. George, 3d Class.   } 𝔘𝔘.
> Wilhelm, 3d Class.   }

CODRINGTON, Sir GEORGE, Rear Admiral, G.C.B.
> St. George, 2d Class.   1828.
> Grand Cross of St. Louis.
> *Battle of Navarino.*

COLBORNE, Sir JOHN, General and K.C.B.
> Maria Theresa.   } 𝔘𝔘.
> St. George, 4th Class. }

COLE, Sir GALBRAITH LOWRY, G.C.B. &c.
> Comm. Tower and Sword.

COLVILLE, Hon. Sir CHARLES, Lieutenant General
and G.C.B.
          † Comm. Tower and Sword. 23 May, 1815.
          P.S.

COMBERMERE, STAPLETON Viscount, G.C.B.
          † Grand Cross Tower and Sword.⎤
             11 March, 1813.   ⎬ P.S.
          Grand Cross Charles III.   ⎥
          Grand Cross St. Fernando.   ⎦

CONGREVE, Sir WILLIAM, Bart.
          St. Anne, 2d Class.
          *Conferred by the Emperor of Russia on account
             of the effect of the Congreve Rockets at the
             Battle of Leipsic, 1813.*

COODE, JOHN, C.B. Captain R.N.
          Comm. of St. Ferdinand and Merit. 6 Nov.
             1818.
          Battle of Algiers.

COOKE, RICHARD HARVEY, Lieutenant Colonel.
          Wladimir, 4th Class. W.

COOKE, Sir GEORGE, Lieutenant General, K.C.B.
          St. George, 3d Class. ⎫
                            ⎬ W.
          Wilhelm, 3d Class.   ⎭

COOKE, HENRY FREDERICK, Colonel, C.B. and
K.C.H.
          St. George, 4th Class.   ⎫
          Military Merit of Prussia. ⎬ 9 March, 1822.
          Kt. Tower and Sword.   ⎭

COOKE, SAMUEL EDWARD, Commander R.N.

    † Kt. Tower and Sword.

    Conferred by the King of Portugal when he went on board H. M. S. the "Windsor Castle," (of which Captain Cooke was first Lieutenant,) in the Tagus, May, 1814.

COOTE, Sir EYRE.   Died 10 Dec. 1823.

    † Crescent.   5 June, 1802.

    Egyptian Campaign, 1801.

CORMICK, JOHN, M.D.

    † Lion and Sun, 2d Class.   30 Aug. 1825.

    † Lion and Sun, 1st Class.   23 April, 1827.

    Services as Physician in the actual service of the Shah of Persia.

COX, Sir WILLIAM, Lieutenant Colonel.   Knighted 1816.

    † Kt. Tower and Sword.   28 Aug. 1815.

    𝔇.𝔖.

CRICHTON, Sir ALEXANDER, M.D.   Knighted 1821.

    † Wladimir, 2d Class.   10 March, 1820.

    Services as First Physician to the Emperor of Russia.

CRICHTON, Sir ARCHIB. WILLIAM.   Knighted 1817.

    St. Anne, 2d Class.

    St. Wladimir.

    Legion of Honour.

CROZIER, RICHARD, Captain R.N.

> † Kt. Tower and Sword.   6 April, 1825.
>
> *Conferred by the King of Portugal when he went on board the "Lively" (of which ship Captain Crozier was then Lieutenant) in the Tagus, May, 1824.*

CROFT, Sir JOHN, Bart.

> † Comm. Tower and Sword.   10 Dec. 1821.

CROSSE, JOSHUA, Major in the Army.

> † St. Fernando.   22 July, 1819.   ⚜.⚜.

CURZON, EDWARD, Captain R.N. and C.B.

> Wladimir.
> St. Louis.   } 1828.
>
> *Battle of Navarino.*

CUST, RICHARD, Captain in the Army.

> Kt. St. Ferdinand and Merit.   21 Oct. 1818.
>
> *Battle of Maida, 1806, and Capture of Ischia and Procida.*

D'ARCY, JOSEPH, Colonel Royal Artillery.

> † Lion and Sun, 2d Class.   16 June, 1818.
> *Services in actual service of the Shah.*

D'ARLEY, WILLIAM, Captain Marines.

> † Kt. of Constantine.   7 Dec. 1801.
> *Services in the Reconquest of Naples, 1799.*

DASHWOOD, Sir CHARLES, Captain R.N. Knighted
20 April, 1825.

† Grand Cross Tower and Sword. 30
March, 1825.

*Conferred when the King of Portugal went on
board H. M. S. " Windsor Castle," in the
Tagus, May, 1824.*

DASHWOOD, CHARLES ROBERT, Lieutenant R.N.

† Kt. Tower and Sword. . 30 March, 1825.

*Conferred when the King of Portugal went on
board H. M. S. " Windsor Castle," in the
Tagus, May, 1824.*

DASHWOOD, JOHN DE COURCY, Lieutenant R.N.

† Kt. Tower and Sword. 30 March, 1825.

*Conferred when the King of Portugal went on
board H. M. S. " Windsor Castle," in the
Tagus, May, 1824.*

D'AUVERGNE, PHILIP, Prince de Bouillon.

† St. Joachim. 27 March, 1807.

DAWSON, Hon. GEORGE LIONEL, Lieutenant Colonel.

Kt. of Maximilian Joseph. ☷.

DE BATHE, WILLIAM PLUNKETT, Major.

† Kt. St. Ferdinand and Merit. 26 June,
1818.

*Services as Aide de Camp to Sir John Stuart,
K. B. at the Battle of Maida and in Sicily.*

De Courcy, Nevinson, Captain R.N.

    † Comm. Tower and Sword. 13 April, 1825.

    Conferred when the King of Portugal went on board H. M. S. " Windsor Castle," in the Tagus, May, 1824.

Devonshire, William Spencer Duke of, K.C.

    † St. Andrew.

    † St. Alexander Newski. } 18 March, 1828.

    † St. Anne.

    Service as Ambassador Extraordinary and Plenipotentiary to St. Petersburgh on occasion of the Coronation of the Emperor Nicholas.

Dick, Sir John, of Braid, N. B. Bart.

    St. Anne of Holstein.

Dick, Robert, Lieutenant Colonel, C.B.

    Maria Theresa.

    Wladimir, 4th Class. } 𝔚𝔄.

Dickinson, Richard, Captain R.N. and C.B.

    St. Louis. 1828.

    Battle of Navarino.

Dornberg, William Baron de, K.C.B. and G.C.H. Major General.

    † St. George. 12 May, 1813. 𝔓.𝔖.

    Wilhelm, 4th Class. 𝔚𝔄.

Douglas, Sir Howard, Bart. Major General and C.B.

    † Kt. Charles III. 30 July, 1813. 𝔓.𝔖.

DOUGLAS, NEIL, Lieutenant Colonel.

Maria Theresa.   } ʊ̃d.
Wladimir, 4th Class. }

DOWNES, ULYSSES Lord, Lieutenant Colonel, K.C.B.

Comm. Tower and Sword.   4 April, 1816.

𝕻.𝕾.

DONOUGHMORE, RICHARD Earl, General.

Crescent.

Egypt.

DOWNIE, Sir JOHN.   Knighted 1813.   Commissary General and Brigadier General in the Portuguese Service.

Small Cross of Charles III. ⎫
    29 April, 1813.   ⎬ 𝕻.𝕾.
Cross of Charles III.   23 ⎪
Sept. 1815.   ⎭

DOYLE, Sir JOHN, Bart. Lieutenant General, G.C.B.

† Crescent.   29 July, 1803.

DOYLE, JOHN MILLEY, Colonel.

† Kt. Tower and Sword.   20 March, 1813.

𝕻.𝕾.

Gazetted as Comm. but was only Kt.

DRUMMOND, Right Hon. WILLIAM, Ambassador to the Ottoman Porte, 1801.

† Crescent.   8 Sept. 1803.

DUMARESQ, PHILIP, Captain R.N.   Died 26 June, 1819.

Sword of Sweden, 4th Class.   10 July, 1813.

DUNCAN, ADAM, Viscount.

      † Alexander Newsky. 5 Dec. 1797.

      Battle of Camperdown.

DUNDAS, Sir ROBERT LAWRENCE, Colonel and K.C.B.

      † Kt. Tower and Sword. 19 Jan. 1814.

      P.S.

D'URBAN, Sir BENJAMIN, K.C.B. and K.C.H. Major General.

      † Comm. Tower and Sword. 21 June, 1814.

      P.S.

DURHAM, Sir PHILIP CHARLES HENDERSON, K.C.B. Vice Admiral of the Red.

      † Comm. of Military Merit of France. 28 June, 1817.

      Capture of Guadaloupe, 1815.

EDGECUMBE, JAMES, Lieutenant R.N.

      Wladimir, 4th Class. 29 Sept. 1815.

      Blockade of Hamburgh.

ELDER, Sir GEORGE, Colonel in the Army, C.B. Knighted 1813.

      † Comm. of Tower and Sword. 20 March, 1813. **P.S**.

ELGIN, THOMAS Earl of.

      † Crescent. 20 March, 1802.

ELLEY, Sir JOHN, K.C.B. Major General.

> Maria Theresa.
> St. George, 4th Class. } ෴.

ELLIOTT, WILLIAM, Captain R.N. C.B.

> † Comm. of Tower and Sword. 30 March,
> 1813.
>
> *Conferred when the King of Portugal went on
> board H. M. S. "Lively," (then commanded
> by Captain E.) in the Tagus, May, 1824.*

ELPHINSTONE, WILLIAM KEITH, Lieutenant Colonel,
C.B.

> St. Anne, 2d Class.
> Wilhelm, 4th Class. } ෴.

ENGLISH, Sir JOHN HAWKER. Knighted 1815.

> † Gustavus Vasa. 5 Oct. 1814.
>
> *Services as Chief Surgeon of the Swedish Army,
> 1813.*

EXMOUTH, EDWARD Viscount, Admiral of the White
and G.C.B.

> † Grand Cross Charles III.
> † Grand Cross St. Ferdinand and
> Merit.
> † Grand Cross St. Maurice and } 3 April,
> St. Lazare.   1817.
> † Grand Cross Wilhelm.
> † Kt. of Annunciation of Savoy.
> *Battle of Algiers.*

FAHIE, WILLIAM CHARLES, Rear Admiral of the Red, K.C.B.

　　† Comm. of St. Ferdinand and Merit.　9 March, 1816.

　　Services as Commander of the British Squadron at the Capture of Gaeta.

FANSHAW, HENRY.

　　† St. George of Russia.　18 July, 1789.

　　Services in the Russian Marine, July, 1789.

　　† Wladimir.　20 March, 1817.

FARQUHAR, ARTHUR, Captain R.N. C.B.

　　† Sword of Sweden.　26 May, 1814.

　　Siege of Gluckstadt.

FELLOWES, THOMAS, Captain R.N. C.B.

　　† Charles III.　22 Feb. 1822.

　　Defence of Cadiz, 1811.

　　St. Anne.

　　Commander of the Legion of Honour. } 1828.

　　Battle of Navarino.

FENWICK, WILLIAM, Lieutenant Colonel, C.B. Lieutenant Governor of Pendennis Castle.

　　† Kt. Tower and Sword.　16 March, 1816.

　　𝔓.𝔖.

FERMOR, Hon. THOMAS WILLIAM, Major General.

　　† Comm. Tower and Sword.　11 May, 1813.

　　𝔓.𝔖.

FIFE, JAMES Earl of.

    † St. Fernando.   6 Feb. 1818.

    Siege of Cadiz and Defence of Fort Mata-gorda, where his Lordship was severely wounded, 1811.

FLEMING, RICHARD H. Commander R.N.

    St. Maurice and Lazare.

    Battle of Algiers, where he commanded the Explosion Vessel.

FLETCHER, Sir RICHARD, Bart. Chief Engineer in Portugal.   Slain at St. Sebastian's, 1813.

    † Comm. Tower and Sword.   11 March, 1813.   ♍♁.

FLIN, JOHN TURNER, Lieutenant R.N.

    † Little Cross of Ferdinand and Merit.   5 March, 1816.

    Services on the Coast of Sicily.

FREMANTLE, Sir THOMAS FRANCIS, Vice Admiral, G.C.B. and G.C.H.   Died 19 Dec. 1819.

    † Comm. of Maria Theresa.   17 May, 1814.

    Services (as Commander of the British Naval Force) with the Austrian Army in the Adriatic Provinces, 1813.

    Grand Cross of Ferdinand and Merit.   2 Jan. 1819.

    Services while commanding the British Squadron in the Adriatic.

FREMANTLE, JOHN, Lieutenant Colonel, C.B.

    Kt. of Maximilian Joseph.   ♍.

GARDINER, Sir ROBERT, Lieutenant Colonel, K.C.B. and K.C.H.

St. Anne, 2d Class. ■■.

GARDNER, Hon. HERBERT, Captain R.A.

† Wladimir, 4th Class. 13 July, 1814.

Siege of Maubeuge. 1814.

GILBERT, ROBERT, Lieutenant Royal Marine Artillery.

† Wladimir, 4th Class. 29 Sept. 1817.

Siege of Dantzic, 1813-14.

GILES, STEPHEN, Lieutenant Marines.

† Kt. Tower and Sword. 5 Oct. 1825.

Conferred when the King of Portugal went on board H. M. S. " Windsor Castle," in the Tagus, May, 1814.

GOMM, Sir WILLIAM, Lieutenant Colonel, K.C.B.

St. Anne, 2d Class. ■■.

GOUGH, Sir HUGH, Colonel and C.B.

† Charles III. 8 Aug. 1815. ■■.

GOSSETT, WILLIAM, Lieutenant Colonel Engineers, C.B.

† Comm. of St. Ferdinand and Merit. 7 March, 1817.

Battle of Algiers.

GRAHAM, COLIN DUNDAS, Lieutenant Colonel.
    † Wilhelm.   10 April, 1818.
    Services while commanding the Scotch Brigade
        formerly in the service of Holland.
GRANT, Sir WILLIAM KEIR, (late KEIR,) Major Ge-
    neral, K.C.B. and K.C.H.
        † Kt. of Maria Theresa.   30 May, 1801.
        Rescue of the Emperor Francis from the French
            Cavalry in Flanders, 24 *April,* 1794.
GRANT, Sir COLQUHOUN, Major General, K.C.B. and
    K.C.H.
        Wladimir, 3d Class. } CH.
        Wilhelm, 3d Class.   }
GRANT, Sir MAXWELL, K.C.B.   Died Oct. 1823.
        † Kt. Tower and Sword.   4 April, 1816.
        P.S.
GREENOCK, CHARLES MURRAY CATHCART Viscount,
    Colonel in the Army.
        Wladimir, 4th Class. } CH.
        Wilhelm, 4th Class.   }
GREIG, Sir JOHN, Vice-Admiral in the Russian Ser-
    vice.
        St. George, 2d Class.
        Conferred 22 Sept. 1770, *for services in action*
            with the Ottoman Fleet.
        St. Anne.   Conferred 25 March, 1774.
        St. Alexander Newskey.   7 July, 1776.
    Registered in Coll. Arm. 1778.

GREEN, ANDREW PELLAT, Captain R.N.
   † Kt. of the Sword.   27 March, 1818.
   Siege of Gluckstadt.
   Kt. of the Iron Crown.
   *Conferred by the Emperor of Austria when he
   went on board H. M. S. "Rochford," (then
   commanded by Captain Green,) at Naples.*

HALKETT, Sir COLIN, Major General, K.C.B. and
   G.C.H.
     Maximilian Joseph. }
     Wilhelm, 3d Class.   }

HALL, ROBERT, Captain R.N.   Knighted 1816.   Died
   7 Feb. 1818.
     † Comm. St. Ferdinand and Merit.   11
     March, 1813.
     *Actions with the Enemy's Flotilla on the Coast
     of Calabria.*

HALLOWELL, Sir BENJAMIN, Vice Admiral of the
   Red and K.C.B.
     † Comm. of St. Ferdinand and Merit.   7
     Jan. 1801.
     *Services in the Reconquest of Naples from the
     French Army, 1799.*

HAMILTON, Sir JOHN, Bart. Lieutenant General.
  † Comm. Tower and Sword. . ⎫
      15 May, 1813.   ⎬ 𝔇.𝔖.
  † Grand Cross Tower and Sword. ⎭
      4 April, 1816.

HAMLEY, WILLIAM, Commander R.N.
  † Leopold. 13 May, 1815.
  *Services at the Siege of Zara, being then First
      Lieutenant of H. M. S. " Havannah."*

HARE, JOHN, Lieutenant Colonel, C.B.
  † Wladimir, 4th Class. 16 March, 1822. 𝔚𝔞.

HARRIS, Hon. WM. GEORGE, Major General.
  Wilhelm, 4th Class. 𝔚𝔞.

HARRIS, THOMAS NOEL, Lieutenant Colonel.
  † Wladimir, 4th Class.   ⎫ 22 Dec. 1814.
  † Military Merit of Prussia. ⎭
  Services with the Allied Armies, 1813-14.

HART, Sir WILLIAM NEVILLE, Chamberlain to Sta-
    nislaus Augustus, King of Poland.
  St. Stanislaus.
  *Said to have been confirmed by Letter of Per-
      mission from the Duke of Portland, Secre-
      tary of State, 1795.*

HARVEY, Sir ROBERT JOHN, Lieutenant Colonel.
  Knighted 1817.
  † Kt. Tower and Sword. 1 May, 1816. 𝔇.𝔖.

HARVEY, WILLIAM MAUNDY, Colonel.
  † Comm. Tower and Sword. 13 May, 1813.
  𝔇.𝔖.

HEATH, JOHN BENJAMIN, Esq. Consul General in London for Sardinia and Genoa.
Kt. of St. Maurice and St. Lazare.

HEPBURN, FRANCIS, Major General and C.B.
Wilhelm, 4th Class.
Wladimir, 4th Class. } 𝔚.

HERTFORD, FRANCIS CHARLES Marquess of.
St. Anne of Russia, 1st Class.   5 July, 1821.
Services while in the actual service of H. I. M. Alexander, during his residence in England.

HERVEY, FELTON ELWILL BATHURST, Colonel and C.B.   Created a Baronet 1818.   Died 24 Sept. 1819.
Kt. Maria Theresa.
Kt. Maximilian Joseph.
St. George, 4th Class. } 𝔚.

HICKS, JOHN, Colonel and C.B.
St. Anne, 2nd Class. 𝔚.

HILL, ROWLAND Lord. G.C.B. G.C.H.
Grand Cross Tower and Sword.   29 April, 1812. 𝔓.𝔖.
Comm. Maria Theresa.
St. George, 2nd Class. } 𝔚.

HILL, Sir DUDLEY ST. LEGER, C.B. 1816.   Knighted 1816.
† Kt. Tower and Sword.   8 Nov. 1816. 𝔓.𝔖.

HILL, Sir THOMAS NOEL, Lieutenant Colonel, K.C.B.
    † Kt. Tower and Sword. 11 March, 1813.
    𝔓.𝔖.
Maximilian Joseph. 𝖂.
HILL, FRANCIS BRIAN, Esq.
    † Tower and Sword. 5 June, 1810.
    *Services as Secretary of Legation at Rio
    Janiero.*
HILL, Sir ROBERT CHAMBRE, Knt. Colonel.
    Maria Theresa.   ⎫
                            ⎬ 𝖂.
    St. George, 4th Class. ⎭
HILL, JOHN, M.D. Died 22 Nov. 1775.
    Gustavus Vasa.
HILLYAR, ROBERT PURKIS, M.D. Surgeon R.N.
    † Kt. Tower and Sword. 6 April, 1815.
    *Conferred when the King of Portugal went on
    board H. M. S. " Windsor Castle," (of which
    Dr. H. was Surgeon,) in the Tagus, May,
    1824.*
HILTON, JOHN, Commander R.N.
    † St. Ferdinand and Merit, 3d Class. 23
    Sept. 1811.
    *Services as First Lieutenant of the " Bustard"
    Sloop of War, in Actions with the Enemy's
    Flotilla near Messina.*
HOOD, SAMUEL, Captain R.N. and G.C.B.   Created a
    Baronet 1809: Died 13 June, 1815.

† Comm. St. Ferdinand and Merit. 7 Jan. 1801.

Re-conquest of Naples from the French Army, 1794.

HOPE, the Right Hon. Sir WILLIAM JOHNSTONE, Vice Admiral of the White and G.C.B.

Malta.

HOPE, Sir GEORGE JOHNSTONE, Rear Admiral and K.C.B. Died 2 May, 1818.

† Sword. 19 July, 1813.

HOSTE, Sir GEORGE CHARLES, Lieutenant Colonel Royal Engineers, C.B.

St. Ferdinand and Merit, 3d Class. 27 Nov. 1811.

Services in an action between H. M. S. "Spartan," and an enemy's squadron, in the Bay of Naples, 3 May, 1810.

HOSTE, WILLIAM, R.N. Created a Bart. 1814. K.C.B.

† Kt. Maria Theresa. 18 May, 1814.

Services in aid of the Austrian Army on the Coast of the Adriatic, 1813.

HOWARD of Effingham, KENNETH ALEXANDER Baron, G.C.B.

† Comm. Tower and Sword. 15 May, 1815.

D.S.

HOWDEN, JOHN FRANCIS Lord, G.C.B.

† Crescent. 15 Dec. 1803.

Egypt.

HUNTE, FRANCIS LE, Commander R.N.
 † Small Cross of St. Ferdinand and Merit.
  14 Nov. 1814.
 Services while Lieutenant R.N. in the action at
  Pietra Nera, 15 Feb. 1813.

JAMIESON, Sir JOHN, Kt. M.D.
 Kt. of Gustavus Vasa.

IMHOFF, Sir CHARLES, Major General.
 † Grand Comm. of St. Joachim. 18 May,
  1807.

JOHNSON, HENRY ALLEN.
 † Wilhelm, 4th Class. 12 Aug. 1817.
 Services as Aide de Camp to the Prince of
  Orange in the Peninsula.

JOHNSTON, EBENEZER, Surgeon R.N.
 † Kt. Tower and Sword. 6 April, 1825.
 Conferred by the King of Portugal when he
  went on board the British Squadron in the
  Tagus, May, 1824, Mr. J. being then Sur-
  geon of H. M. S. " Liberty."

JONES, Sir HARFORD, (now Sir HARFORD JONES
 BRYDGES.) Created a Baronet 1807.
 † Crescent. 24 May, 1804.
 † Crescent, superior order. 5 March, 1807.

JONES, JAMES, Major.
> † Charles III.   6 Sept. 1816.
> *Battles of Barrosa and Castulla.*

JONES, BENJAMIN ORLANDO, Major.
> † Tower and Sword.   17 Dec. 1827.   𝔓.𝔖.

KEIR.   (See GRANT.)

KEITH, GEORGE Viscount, G.C.B. &c.
> † Crescent.   20 March, 1802.
> *Egypt.*
> † Grand Cross St. Maurice
>   and St. Lazare.   } 1 Aug. 1822.
> *Bombardment of Genoa,* 1800.

KELLIE, THOMAS Earl of.   Died 6 Feb. 1828.
> † Comm. of Vasa.   6 July, 1808.

KELLY, EDWARD, Major.
> St. Anne, 2d Class.   𝔚𝔲.

KEMPT, Sir JAMES, Major General, G.C.B. and G.C.H.
> Maria Theresa.
> St. George, 2d Class.   } 𝔚𝔲.
> Wilhelm, 3d Class.   }

KNOLLES, HENRY, Lieutenant R.N.
> † Kt. of the Tower and Sword.   20 April,
>   1825.
> *Conferred by the King of Portugal when he
>   went on board H. M. S. " Windsor Castle,"
>   in the Tagus, May,* 1824.

H

LAWRENCE, Sir THOMAS, President of the Royal Aca-
demy.
    † Legion of Honour.   10 July, 1826.
LAMBERT, Sir JOHN, Lieutenant General, K.C.B.
        Wladimir, 3d Class.   } <i>ea.</i>
        Maximilian Joseph.   }
LEE, Sir RICHARD, Vice Admiral, K.C.B.
        Comm. Tower and Sword.   31 May, 1815.
        ℔.℔.
LEITH, Sir JAMES, Lieutenant General, G.C.B. Died
    at Barbadoes, 16 Oct. 1816.
        † Comm. Tower and Sword.   19 Jan. 1814.
        ℔.℔.
        † Grand Cordon of Military Merit of France.
        20 Nov. 1816.
        Capture of Guadaloupe, August, 1815.
LEMOINE, JOHN, Colonel Royal Artillery and C.B.
        † Comm. of St. Ferdinand and Merit.   15
        Aug. 1816.
        Battle of Maida, Repulse of the enemy from
        Messina, 18 Sept. 1816.
LINDENTHAL, LEWIS, Lieutenant General.
        Crescent.
        Egypt.

LINDSAY, THOMAS, Major E.I.C.S.
>> Lion and Sun, 1st Class. 2 June, 1820.

LONDONDERRY, CHARLES WILLIAM Marquess of,
G.C.B. and G.C.H.
>> Comm. Tower and Sword. 27 March, 1813.
>> D.S.
>> Grand Cross of the Sword.
>> St. George, 4th Class.
>> Black Eagle of Prussia. } 22 March, 1814.
>> Red Eagle of Prussia.
>> *Services in the Campaign of 1813, especially at the Battles of Culm and Leipsic.*

LOUIS, Sir THOMAS, Rear Admiral. Created a Baronet 1806. Died 17 May, 1807.
>> † Comm. of Ferdinand and Merit. 19 April, 1802.
>> Kt. of Maria Theresa.
>> *Services in the Re-conquest of Naples from the French, 1799.*

LOWE, Sir HUDSON, Major General. K.C.B.
>> St. George, 2d Class.

LYON, Sir JAMES, Major General, K.C.B. G.C.H.
>> Kt. of the Sword. 1 June, 1814.
>> † Comm. of the Sword. 8 May, 1817.
>> *Campaign of 1813, in Germany.*
>> Comm. of Maximilian Joseph. BM.

MACARTNEY, GEORGE Earl.   Died 1806.
    White Eagle of Poland.

MACBEAN, WILLIAM, Colonel.
    † Kt. Tower and Sword.   24 March, 1813.
    P.S.

MAC CREAGH, MICHAEL, Lieutenant Colonel and
    C.B.
    Kt. Tower and Sword.
      20 May, 1816.   } P.S.
    † Comm. Tower and Sword.
      28 Dec. 1821.

McCORMICK, JOHN, M.D.
    † Lion and Sun, 2d Class.   20 Sept. 1815.
    Services in the actual service of the Shah.

MACDONALD, ALEXANDER, Colonel Royal Artillery
    and C.B.
    † St. Anne, 2d Class.   25 Feb. 1815.
    Siege of Dantzick, 1814.

MACDONALD, ALEXANDER, Colonel Royal Artillery.
    St. Anne, 2d Class.   W.I.

MACDONELL, JAMES, Colonel and C.B.
    Maria Theresa.   } W.I.
    Wladimir, 4th Class.

MACFARLANE, ROBERT, Lieutenant General, G.C.H.
    † Grand Cross of St. Ferdinand and Merit.
      20 Jan. 1817.
    Service in Italy, and especially at the Capture
      of Genoa, 1814.

Mᶜ GRIGOR, Sir JAMES, M.D.   Knighted 1814.
    † Comm. Tower and Sword.   3 April, 1816.
    𝕭.𝕾.

MACKENZIE, Sir ALEXANDER, Bart. General and
    G.C.H.
    † Grand Cross St. Januarius.   14 May, 1818.
    *Services in Sicily, 1808-9 and 10, especially at
        the capture of Scylla and occupation of
        Lower Calabria.*

MACKENZIE, KENNETH, Captain R.N.   Died about
    1826.
    † Kt. of the Sword.   11 Feb. 1815.
    Blockade of Norway, 1813-14.

MACHLACHLAN, ALEXANDER, Captain R. Artillery.
    † St. Maurice and St. Lazare.   1 Aug. 1816.
    *Services while commanding an Artillery Corps
        of the Italian Levy on the East Coast of
        Spain, 1813 and 14.*

MACLAINE, ARCHIBALD, Lieutenant Colonel, C.B.
    Charles III.   12 Oct. 1816.
    *Defence of Fort Matagorda, 1810, Battle of
        Barrosa, Capture of Seville, 1812.*

MACLEAN, CHARLES, M.D.
    Charles III.   29 July, 1823.
    Services in the Spanish service.

MACLEAN, Sir JOHN, Major General and K.C.B.
    † Kt. Tower and Sword.   15 May, 1815.
    𝕭.𝕾.

MACLEOD, HENRY GEORGE, Major.
† Wladimir, 4th Class. 13 Feb. 1815.
Siege of Dantzick, 1813.

MADDEN, GEORGE ALAN, Major General, C.B.
Crescent.
Egypt.
† Comm. Tower and Sword. 4 April, 1816.
P.S.

MAITLAND, Sir PEREGRINE, Major General, K.C B.
Wladimir, 4th Class. } W.
Wilhelm, 3d Class. }

MALCOLM, Sir JOHN, Major General, G.C.B.
† Lion and Sun. 22 Sept. 1812.
Services as Ambassador from India to Persia.

MANSELL, THOMAS, Captain R.N.
Sword, 4th Class. 28 June, 1813.

MARKLAND, JOHN DUFF, Captain R.N. C.B.
† Leopold. 5 March, 1816.
Siege of Trieste; and services during the campaign of 1813-14, *in Italy.*

MARSHALL, JOHN, Captain R.N. C.B.
† Kt. of the Sword. } 24 Dec. 1814.
† St. George, 4th Class. }
Blockade of Hamburgh and Siege of Gluckstadt, 1813-14.

MARTIN, Sir GEORGE, Vice Admiral, G.C.B.
Grand Cross St. Januarius. 6 July, 1811.
Services as Commander-in-Chief on the Coast of Sicily.

MARTIN, Sir THOMAS BYAM, Vice Admiral, K.C.B.
    Sword.

MAY, Sir JOHN, Lieutenant Colonel Royal Artillery,
    K.C.B. and K.C.H.
        † Kt. Tower and Sword.   15 May, 1815.
        𝔓.𝔖.
        St. Anne, 2d Class.   𝔘𝔦.

MENDS, Sir ROBERT, Captain R.N.   Knighted 1815.
    Died 1824.
        Charles III.   16 May, 1815.
        Services while commanding the British Squadron
        on the Coasts of Gallicia and Cantabria.

MERTON, HORATIO Viscount.   Only son of Earl
    Nelson.   Died January, 1808.
        † St. Joachim.   25 April, 1806.

MILES, Sir EDWARD, Kt. Lieutenant Colonel, C.B.
        † Kt. Tower and Sword.   6 April, 1820.
        𝔓.𝔖.

MILNE, Sir DAVID, Vice Admiral, K.C.B.
        † St. Januarius.   } 3 Oct. 1820.
        † Comm. Wilhelm. .
    Battle of Algiers.

MITCHELL, HENRY, Colonel and C.B.
        St. Anne, 2d Class.   } 𝔘𝔦.
        Wladimir, 3d Class.

MONTAGUE, WILLOUGHBY, Lieut. Royal Artillery.
        † Wladimir, 4th Class.   21 April, 1815.
    Siege of Dantzick.

MONTEITH, WILLIAM, Captain of Engineers E.I.C.S.
    Lion and Sun, 2d Class.
    Services in actual service of the Shah.

MOODY, THOMAS, Major Engineers.
    † Kt. of Military Merit of France.   28 April,
    1820.
    Capture of Guadaloupe, August, 1815.

MOORMAN, RICHARD, Commander R.N.
    † Ferdinand and Merit, Small Cross.   4
    March, 1813.
    Actions near Messina.

MORESBY, FAIRFAX, Captain R.N. C.B.
    † Kt. of Maria Theresa.   18 May, 1814.
    *Services with the Austrian Army on the Coast
    of the Adriatic, 1813.*

MULCASTER, W. H. Captain R.N. and C.B.
    † Tower and Sword.   30 Sept. 1825.
    Capture of Cayenne.

MULLER, HENRY FREDERICK, Colonel.
    Kt. of Military Merit of Wirtumburg.
    1 Oct. 1825.

MURRAY, Sir JOHN, Bart. Lieutenant General, G.C.H.
    St. Januarius.
    *Services while commanding in Sicily, and at the
    Battle of Castalla in Spain.*

MURRAY, Sir GEORGE, Lieutenant General, G.C.B.
    and G.C.H.
    Crescent.
    Egypt.

† Comm. Tower and Sword.   6 May, 1813.
𝔇.𝔖.

† Grand Cross Leopold.
† Grand Cross Alexander Newsky.
† Grand Cross Red Eagle of Prussia.
† Comm. Maximilian Joseph.
† Comm. St. Henry of Saxony.
   16 Sept. 1825.

} 𝔇.𝔖.

MUTTLEBURY, GEORGE, Lieutenant Colonel, C.B.
   Wilhelm, 4th Class.   𝔚𝔦.

MUTER.   (See STRATON.)

NAYLER, Sir GEORGE, Kt. Garter P. K. of A. &c.
   † Comm. Tower and Sword.   5 June, 1824.
   *Investing the King of Portugal with the Order
   of the Garter.*

NELSON, HORATIO Viscount, and Duke of Bronte in
   Sicily.
      † Grand Cross Ferdinand and Merit. (Be-
      ing the first nominated, Suvarroff the Se-
      cond, and the Emperor Paul, the Third.)
      9 Jan. 1801.
      † Crescent.   20 March, 1802.
      † Grand Comm. of St. Joachim.   15 July,
      1802.
   Battle of the Nile.

NICOLAS, JOHN TOUP, Captain R.N. and C.B.

    Kt. of St. Ferdinand and Merit.

    † Comm. of St. Ferdinand and Merit.   12 Oct. 1816.

    Services while Captain of H. M. S. " Pilot," on the Coast of Calabria, 1810-11 and 12.

NIXON, ROBERT, Lieutenant Colonel.

    Wladimir, 4th Class. } vel.
    Wilhelm, 4th Class.

NORCOTT, AMOS GODSILL ROBERT, Colonel and C.B.

    Maximilian Joseph. } vel.
    St. Anne, 2d Class.

OAKES, Sir HILDEBRAND, Baronet.   Died 9 Sept. 1822.

    Crescent.

    Egypt.

OTWAY, Sir LOFTUS WILLIAM, Major General and C.B.

    † Charles III. 9 May, 1816. P.S.

OUGHTON, GEORGE VOLLER, Purser R.N.

    † Kt. Tower and Sword. 21 April, 1825.

    Conferred when the King of Portugal went on board the British Squadron in the Tagus, May, 1824.

OUSELY, Sir GORE, Bart.
>Lion and Sun.
>St. George, 2d Class.
>Alexander Newsky.
>Wladimir, 4th Class.

PACK, Sir DENIS, Major General, K.C.B. Died 24 July, 1823.
>† Comm. Tower and Sword. 11 March, 1813. **P.S.**
>Wladimir, 4th Class. } **Vï.**
>Maria Theresa.

PAGE, ROBERT, of Madeira.
>Kt. Tower and Sword.

PAGET, Hon. Sir EDWARD, Lieutenant General, G.C.B.
>† Grand Cross Tower and Sword. 29 April, 1812. **P.S.**

PAKENHAM, Sir EDWARD MICHAEL, G.C.B. Slain at New Orleans, 8 Jan. 1815.
>† Comm. Tower and Sword. 5 Jan. 1814. **P.S.**

PARKER, EDWARD AUGUSTUS, Lieutenant R.M.
>† Kt. Tower and Sword. 26 Sept. 1825.
>*Conferred when the King of Portugal went on board H. M. S. "Windsor Castle," in the Tagus, May, 1824.*

PARRY, WILLIAM HENRY WEBLEY, (late Webly,)
 Captain R.N. and C.B.
  † Grand Cross of the Sword. 19 Jan. 1809.
  Services as Captain of H. M. S. " Centaur,"
   in action with the Russian Fleet, 26 Aug.
   1808.

PEACOCK, THOMAS, Major.
  † Kt. Tower and Sword. 24 Oct. 1825.

PEACOCKE, WARREN MARMADUKE, Major General.
 Knighted 1815.
 Crescent.
 Egypt.
  † Comm. Tower and Sword. 24 May, 1815.
  P.S.

PEAT, Rev. Sir ROBERT, D.D.
  † St. Stanislaus. 2 Oct. 1804.

PENROSE, Sir CHARLES VINICOMBE, Vice Admiral,
 K.C.B. and G.C.M.G.
  † Grand Cross of St. Ferdinand and Merit.
  12 Aug. 1819.
  Services while commanding the British Squa-
  dron against Gaeta, 1815.

PERCIVAL, WESTBY, Captain R.N.
 Leopold. 5 March, 1816.
 Siege of Trieste and Campaign of 1813-14 in
 Italy.

PETER, JOHN, of the Exchequer Bill Office.
 Grand Cross of Merit of Holstein, 1782.

PHILLIPS, Sir CHARLES, Knight, Major General.
Knighted 1817.

† Grand Cross of St. Januarius.   20 Jan.
1817.

Defence of Sicily and Expedition to Italy, 1815.

PICTON, Sir THOMAS, G.C.B.   Slain at Waterloo.

† Comm. Tower and Sword.   19 Oct. 1813.
𝔇.𝔖.

PITTS, EDWARD, Lieutenant R.N.

† Kt. Tower and Sword.   7 May, 1825.

*Conferred by the King of Portugal when he
went on board H. M. S. the " Windsor
Castle," in the Tagus, May,* 1824.

POCKLINGTON, Sir ROBERT.

† Maria Theresa.   30 May, 1801.

*Rescuing the Emperor of Germany from the
French Cavalry,* 1794.

POE, EMANUEL, Captain in the Army.   Died about
1823.

Charles III.   20 May, 1816.   𝔇.𝔖.

PONSONBY, Hon. FREDERICK CAVENDISH, Major
General and C.B.

† Kt. Tower and Sword.   28 Feb. 1814.
𝔇.𝔖.

Maria Theresa.
St. George, 4th Class.   } 𝔴𝔞.

POPHAM, Sir HOME RIGGS, Adm.   Died 11 Sept. 1820.

† Comm. St. John of Jerusalem.   20 Sept.
1799.

PORTER, Sir ROBERT KERR.   Knighted 1813.
St. Joachim.
Lion and Sun.

POWER, Sir MANLEY, K.C.B. Major General.   Died
1825.
† Comm. Tower and Sword.   15 June, 1825.
P.S.

PYNN, Sir HENRY, Lieut. Colonel, C.B.   Knighted
1815.
† Kt. Tower and Sword.   17 Jan. 1815.
† Comm. Tower and Sword.   16 July, 1822.
P.S. and especially at the Battle of the Pyrenees.

RAINS, WILLIAM KINGDOM, Captain Royal Artillery.
† Leopold.   9 Oct. 1815.
Italian Campaign, 1813-14.

READE, Sir THOMAS, Lieutenant Colonel, C.B.
Knighted 1825.
† Small Cross of St. Ferdinand and Merit.
30 Jan. 1813.
Services near Messina, 1810, being then Assistant Quarter Master General of the Forces in Sicily.

REYNELL, THOMAS, Major General.
> Maria Theresa.
> St. George, 4th Class. } out.

ROBE, Sir WILLIAM, Colonel, K.C.B. and K.C.H.
Died 1 Nov. 1820.
> † Comm. Tower and Sword. 25 Jan. 1815.
> 𝔇.𝔖.

ROBERTS, RICHARD, Lieutenant Colonel.
> † St. Maurice and St. Lazare. 17 June,
> 1817.
> *Siege of Genoa, 1814.*

ROBERTSON, GEORGE DUNCAN, Major General, C.B.
> † Leopold. 5 March, 1816.
> *Siege of Trieste and Campaign in Italy,*
> *1813-14.*

ROBINSON, WILLIAM, Lieutenant Colonel Royal Marine Artillery, C.B.
> † Comm. of St. Ferdinand and Merit. 23
> Sept. 1823.
> *Defence of Sicily while Commander of the*
> *Combined Flotilla.*

ROCHE, Sir PHILIP KEATING, C.B. K.C.H. Knighted 1816.
> † Charles III.
> † St. Fernando, 3d Class. } 𝔇.𝔖.
> 15 March, 1816.

ROLT, JOHN, Lieutenant Colonel, C.B.
> † Kt. Tower and Sword. 28 Nov. 1816.
> 𝔇.𝔖.

ROSE, JAMES, Captain R.N.
        † Sword.   6 Feb. 1815.
        Siege of Gluckstadt.
ROSS, ARCHIBALD, Lieutenant Colonel.
        † Kt. Tower and Sword.   3 May, 1816.   𝔓.𝔖.
ROSS, JOHN, Captain R.N.
        † Sword, 4th Class.   4 Dec. 1813.   𝔓.𝔖.
ROSS, Sir HEW DALRYMPLE, Lieutenant Colonel,
    K.C.B.
        † Kt. Tower and Sword.   16 May, 1815.
        𝔓.𝔖.
        St. Anne, 2d Class.   𝔘𝔘.
ROSS, JOHN, Colonel and C.B.
        Wilhelm, 4th Class.   } 𝔘𝔘.
        Wladimir, 4th Class.   }
ROWLEY, CHARLES, Vice Admiral and K.C.B.
        † Kt. of Maria Theresa.   28 May, 1814.
        Campaign in Italy, 1813-14.
RUMFORD, Count.   See THOMPSON.
RYAN, Sir EDWARD MICHAEL.
        † Maria Theresa.   30 May, 1801.
        *Rescuing the Emperor of Germany from the
        French Cavalry, 1794.*

SADLER, FREDERICK WILLIAM RICHARD, Master R.N.:

> † Kt. Tower and Sword. 30 March, 1825.
> *Conferred when the King of Portugal went on board H. M. S. the " Windsor Castle," (of which Mr. S. was then Master,) in the Tagus, May, 1824.*

ST. VINCENT, JOHN Earl of, G.C.B. &c.

> † Grand Cross Tower and Sword. 15 Sept. 1817.
> *Services rendered to the Kingdom of Portugal.*

SALTOUN, ALEXANDER GEORGE Lord, Col. and C.B.

> Maria Theresa.
> St. George, 4th Class. } ☙.

SAUMAREZ, Sir JAMES, Bart. and K.B.

> † Grand Cross of the Sword. 4 May, 1813.
> Invested with the Insignia of that Order by H. R. H. the Prince Regent, at Carlton House, 24 June, 1813.

SAUMAREZ, RICHARD, Captain R.N.

> Leopold. 28 April, 1821.
> *Campaign of 1813-14, in Italy.*

SCHOMBERG, CHARLES MARSH, Captain R.N. C.B.

> † Comm. Tower and Sword. 30 Aug. 1815.
> 𝕯.𝕾.

SCOVELL, Sir GEORGE, Colonel and K.C.B.

> Wladimir, 4th Class. ☙.

SEATON, JOHN, Lieutenant R.N.

> † Kt. Tower and Sword. 6 April, 1825.

I

Conferred when the King of Portugal went on board the British Squadron in the Tagus, May, 1824, Mr. S. being then Lieutenant of H. M. S. " Lively."

SILVESTRE, THOMAS, Surgeon of H. M. S. Confiance.

    † Kt. Tower and Sword.   7 April, 1810.

Care of the Portuguese Sick and Wounded at Cayenne.

SHEARMAN, JOHN, Captain in the Army.

    † Kt. of St. Maurice and St. Lazare.   2 April, 1816.

Services as Brigade Major of the Italian Levy.

SILVERTOP, CHARLES, Captain in the Army.

    Charles III.   30 July, 1816.

    P.S. especially at Barrosa and Usagre.

SHARPE, ROBERT, Commander R.N.

    † Kt. Tower and Sword.   11 April, 1826.

Conferred when the King of Portugal went on board H. M. S. " Windsor," (of which Mr. S. was then Lieutenant,) in the Tagus, May, 1824.

SMITH, Sir CHARLES FELIX, Lieutenant Colonel Engineers.   Knighted 1814.

    † Charles III.   16 Sept. 1814.

Defence of Tarifa, 1811.

SMITH, CHARLES HAMILTON, Major.

    Wilhelm, 4th Class.   10 June, 1823.

Taking of Zeirickzee and the Island of Zealand.

SMITH, Sir WILLIAM SYDNEY, Admiral.

> † Comm. and Grand Cross of the Sword, with the Insignia of which he was invested by his late Majesty at St. James's Palace.
>
> *Services at Toulon*, 1793 and 4.
>
> Crescent, 1st Class.
>
> *Egypt and Syria*, 1799.
>
> † Grand Cross St. Ferdinand and Merit. 28 July, 1807.
>
> *Egypt and Syria*, 1799.
>
> Grand Cross Tower and Sword.
>
> Kt. of St. John of Jerusalem.

SMYTH, Sir JAMES CARMICHAEL, Bart. Major General and C.B.

> Maria Theresa.
> Wladimir, 4th Class. } ₥.

SMYTH, WILLIAM HENRY, Captain R.N.

> † Small Cross St. Ferdinand and Merit. 16 March, 1816.
>
> *Services off Messina*, 1810.

SOMERSET, Lord FITZROY, Colonel, K.C.B.

> Comm. Tower and Sword. ₪.₪.
>
> St. George, 4th Class.
> Maximilian Joseph.   } ₥.
> Maria Theresa.
> 4 April, 1816.

SOMERSET, Lord ROBERT EDWARD HENRY, Major
    General, K.C.B.
        † Tower and Sword.   11 March, 1813.
        𝔓𝔖.
        Maria Theresa.   } 𝔳𝔦𝔦.
        Wladimir, 3d Class.   }

SOMERVILLE, JOHN, Lieutenant R.N.
        † Kt. Tower and Sword.   6 April, 1825.
        *Conferred when the King of Portugal went- on
            board the " Windsor Castle," (of which Mr.
            S. was a Lieutenant,) in the Tagus, May,
            1824.*

SOUZA, MICHAEL DE.
        † Christ.   7 Jan. 1805.
        *Services rendered to the Portuguese Govern-
            ment at Goa.*

SPENCER, Hon. FREDERICK, Captain R.N.
        St. Louis.   } 1828.
        St. Anne.   }
        Battle of Navarino.

SPENCER, Sir BRENT, General, G.C.B.
        † Grand Cross Tower and Sword.   29 April,
            1812. 𝔓𝔖.

STAINES, Sir THOMAS, K.C.B. Captain R.N.
        † Comm. St. Ferdinand and Merit.   17
            Nov. 1809.
        *Action between H. M. S. " Cyane," and a
            Neapolitan Flotilla, 27 June, 1809.*

STAPLETON, JOHN CHARLES, late Officer of Cuirassiers in the Royal Prussian Guard.

    † Kt. of St. John of Prussia. 22 April, 1822.

    Services while in the actual service of the King of Prussia.

STEELE, Sir ROBERT, Lieutenant of Marines, and Colonel in the Spanish service. Knighted 1817.

    † Charles III. 15 Aug. 1816.

    Pensioned Kt. of Charles III. 19 Oct. 1819.

    P.S. *especially at the Passage of the Bidassoa and Battles of the Pyrenees*, 1813.

STEWART, Hon. Sir WILLIAM, Lieutenant General, G.C.B. Died 7 Jan. 1827.

    † Comm. Tower and Sword. 5 Jan. 1814.

    P.S.

STOPFORD, Hon. Sir EDWARD, Lieutenant General, K.C.B.

    † Comm. Tower and Sword. 10 Feb. 1814.

    P.S.

STORY, GEORGE, Captain in the Army.

    † Wladimir, 4th Class. 7 May, 1815. **P.S.**

STRACHEY, CHRISTOPHER, Captain R.N.

    Wladimir, 4th Class. 20 March, 1820.

    Defence of Dantzic, 1807.

STRANGFORD, PERCY-CLINTON SYDNEY Viscount, G.C.B. and G.C.H.

    Grand Cross Tower and Sword.

...

... ...

... ...

... ... X

... ...

... ...

... ...

... ...

... ...

... ...

... ...

... ...

... ... 24 Sept. ...

... ... Feb. 1814. ...

...ILL... ... Sir W...... Major General and C.B. William and Sword **...**

...ILL... ... Sir WILLIAM. Brigadier General in the Portuguese Army.
 ✦ Comm. Tower and Sword. 16 Feb. 181...
 D.S.

WILLIAMS, KELLET HENRY. Lieutenant Colonel. Killed at Baigorre in France, March, 1814, three days before the Battle of Toulouse.
 ✦ Kt. Tower and Sword. 19 Jan. 1814.
 D.S.

SYDENHAM, THOMAS. Died at Lisbon, 28 Aug. 1816.
> St. George, 4th Class.
> Sword.
> *Services with the Swedish Army, 1813.*

SUTTON, Sir CHARLES, K.C.B. Died 26 March, 1828.
> Comm. Tower and Sword.

TEMPLE, EDMUND, Captain in the Spanish Army.
> † Charles III. 6 July, 1816.
> **P.S.** *and especially at Arroyo del Puerco, Caçeres, Arroyo de Molino, and Passage of the Bidassoa.*

THESIGER, FREDERICK, Captain R.N. and late Captain in the Russian Navy. Died 2 Sept. 1805.
> † St. George, 4th Class. 27 Oct. 1803.
> *Action with the Swedish Fleet, 22 June, 1790.*

THOMPSON, HENRY CLEMENTS, Commander R.N.
> † Kt. Sword of Sweden. 6 Jan. 1809.
> *Action with the Russian Fleet, 26 Aug. 1808.*

THOMPSON, Sir BENJAMIN Count RUMFORD. Died 1814.
> † White Eagle. } 4 Jan. 1794.
> St. Stanislaus. }

THORNTON, Sir EDWARD, G.C.B.

> Conde di Cassilhas in Portugal.   10 Oct.
> 1825.

TORRENS, Sir HENRY, Major General, K.C.B.

> † Comm. Tower and Sword.   15 March,
> 1821. 𝕻.𝕾.

TORRENS, ROBERT, Lieutenant Colonel, C.B.

> St. Anne, 2d Class. 𝕽𝖆.

TRANT, Sir NICHOLAS, Captain of Staff Corps, and
sometime Governor of Oporto.

> † Comm. Tower and Sword.   18 Oct. 1811.
> 𝕻.𝕾.

TRAVERS, Sir ROBERT, Major General and C.B.

> † Comm. St. Ferdinand and Merit.   13
> Nov. 1816.

> *Services while with the Anglo-Sicilian Army on
> the Coast of Italy.*

TRENCH, The Hon. Sir ROBERT LE POER, K.C.B.
Colonel in the Army.   Died March, 1824.

> Kt. Tower and Sword. 7 Dec. 1815. 𝕻.𝕾.

TROWBRIDGE, Sir THOMAS, Bart.   Lost at sea, 1805.

> † Comm. Ferdinand and Merit.   7 Jan.
> 1801.

> *Reconquest of Naples,* 1799.

TULLOH, ALEXANDER, Lieutenant Colonel Royal
Artillery, C.B.

> † Kt. Tower and Sword.   5 April, 1816.
> 𝕻.𝕾.

TURNER, Sir HILGROVE, Lieutenant General, K.C.H.
>   Crescent.
>   *Egypt.*
>   St. Anne of Russia.

TYRWHITT, Sir THOMAS, Gentleman Usher of the
>   Black Rod.
>   † St. Anne, 1st Class.   11 Sept. 1824.
>   *Assisting at the Investiture of the Emperor of*
>   *Russia with the Order of the Garter, at*
>   *Toplitz, 1813.*

VANDELEUR, Sir JOHN ORMSBY, Lieutenant General,
>   K.C.B.
>   Maximilian Joseph.   } 🕮.
>   Wladimir, 2d Class.

VERE, Sir CHARLES BROOKE, Lieutenant Colonel
>   K.C.B. K.C.H.
>   † Kt. Tower and Sword. } ℗.♄.
>   16 May, 1815.
>   Wladimir, 4th Class.   } 🕮.
>   Wilhelm, 4th Class.

VIVIAN, Sir ROBERT HUSSEY, Bart. Major General,
>   K.C.B. K.C.H.
>   Maria Theresa.   } 🕮.
>   Wladimir, 4th Class.

UPTON, Hon. ARTHUR PERCY, Major General and C.B.

    † Maximilian Joseph.   7 Oct. 1816.

    Services while attached to the Bavarian Army, 1815, and especially at the Passage of the Saare, 23 June.

WALKER, Sir GEORGE TOWNSHEND, Lieutenant General, G.C.B.

    † Comm. Tower and Sword.   18 May, 1815.

    P.S.

WALKER, JAMES, Rear Admiral, C.B.

    † Comm. Tower and Sword.   30 April, 1816.

    P.S.

WALKER, WILLIAM, Lieutenant R.N.

    † Kt. Tower and Sword.   30 March, 1825.

    Conferred when the King of Portugal went on board the " Windsor Castle," (of which Mr. W. was Lieutenant,) in the Tagus, May, 1824.

WARRE, WILLIAM, Lieutenant Colonel.

    † Kt. Tower and Sword.   9 April, 1816.

    P.S.

WARREN, Sir JOHN BORLASE, Admiral, Bart. G.C.B. Died 1822.

    † Crescent.   21 August, 1802.

WATERS, JOHN, Colonel, C.B.

      St. Anne, 2d Class. 𝕎.

WATSON, Sir HENRY, Lieutenant Colonel.

      † Kt. Tower and Sword. 11 March, 1816.
      𝔓.𝔖.

WAVELL, ARTHUR GOODALL, Colonel in the Spanish
Service.

      † Charles III.
      † St. Fernando. } 16 Feb. 1818.

      Assault on the French Lines before Tarragona,
         16 June, 1811.

WAY, Sir GREGORY HOLMAN BROMLEY, Lieutenant
Colonel, C.B.

      † Kt. Tower and Sword. 11 March, 1813.
      𝔓.𝔖.

WELLESLEY, RICHARD Marquess, K.G.

      † Crescent. 16 Nov. 1805.
      † Sun and Lion. 29 July, 1812.

WELLINGTON, ARTHUR Duke of, K.G. G.C.B. and
G.C.H.

      Prince of Waterloo in the Netherlands.

      Duke of Ciudad Rodrigo, and Grandee of
         Spain, of the First Class.

      Duke of Vittoria, Marquess of Torres Vedras,
         and Count of Vimiera, in Portugal.

      † Grand Cross Maria Theresa. 4 March,
      1814.

      † Grand Cross Tower and Sword. 19 Oct.
      1811.

    † Grand Cross Sword of Sweden. 4 March, 1814.

    † Grand Cross St. Ferdinand and Merit. 16 July, 1817.

    † Grand Cross St. Januarius. 16 July, 1817.

    Golden Fleece.

    St. Esprit.

    Elephant.

    Grand Cross St. Férnando.

    Grand Cross St. George of Russia.

    Grand Cross Black Eagle.

    Grand Cross Wilhelm.

    Grand Cross Annunciade of Savoy.

    Grand Cross Maximilian Joseph.

    Grand Cross Military Merit of Bavaria.

WEST, Sir AUGUSTUS, Physician to the King of Portugal. Knighted 24 Nov. 1824.

    † Comm. Tower and Sword. 28 Oct. 1824.

WESTERN, THOMAS, Rear Admiral.   Died 26 Dec. 1814.

    † Comm. Tower and Sword. 26 Aug. 1814.

WHITTINGHAM, Sir SAMUEL FORD, Kt. Major General, C.B. and K.C.H.

    † St. Fernando. 9 May, 1815.

    † Grand Cross of the same. 3 Nov. } P.S.
    1815.

WILLES, GEORGE WICKENS, Captain R.N.

    ↑ Small Cross of St. Ferdinand and Merit, 3d Class. 26 June, 1812.

Services as First Lieutenant of H. M. S. "Spartan," in action with a French Squadron before Naples, 3 May, 1810.

WILLIAMS, Sir JAMES, Colonel in the Austrian service, and Commander of the Imperial Flotillas on the Adriatic, the Italian Lakes, and the Danube, in 1796 and 1799.

Maria Theresa.

WILLIAMS, Sir EDMUND KEYNTON, Lieutenant Colonel, K.C.B.

    † Kt. Tower and Sword. 4 April, 1816. 𝔓.𝔖.

WILLIAMS, Sir WILLIAM, Colonel, K.C.B.

    † Kt. Tower and Sword. 11 March, 1813. 𝔓.𝔖.

WILLOCK, Sir HENRY, Major E.I.C.S. Knighted 1827.

    † Lion and Sun. 3 July, 1826.

WILLOCK, GEORGE, Major E.I.C.S.

    † Lion and Sun. 23 April, 1827.

WILSON, Sir JOHN, Kt. Colonel, C.B.

    † Comm. Tower and Sword. 11 March, 1813. 𝔓.𝔖.

WILSON, Sir ROBERT THOMAS.

    † Kt. Maria Theresa. 2 June, 1801.

Rescuing the Emperor of Germany from the French Cavalry, 1794.

    † Comm. of Maria Theresa. 4 March, 1814.

    † St. George, 3d Class. 31 Dec. 1813.

*Conferred by the Emperor Alexander in person,
in presence of the Russian Army in the Camp
of Jauer, 27 May, 1813, for his services
during the Campaigns 1812–13.*

† Comm. Tower and Sword. ⎱ ℙ.𝔖.
　　19 Oct. 1811. ⎰

† Red Eagle of Prussia.　4 March, 1814.

† St. Anne, 1st Class.　23 July, 1814.

＊ These Orders were all resumed by the Emperors of
Russia and Austria, and Kings of Prussia and Portugal, in 1821.

WISHART, JAMES LOCKHART.
　　Count of the H. R. E. and Knight of Maria
　　　Theresa.　14 May, 1785.

WOOD, Sir GEORGE ADAM, Kt. Colonel Royal Artil-
　　lery, C.B. and K.C.H.
　　　Maria Theresa.
　　　Wladimir, 4th Class. ⎱
　　　Wilhelm, 3d Class. ⎰ 𝔒𝔘.
　　　25 May, 1820.

WOOD, CHARLES, Major.
　　† Prussian Order of Military Merit.　14 Feb.
　　1815.
　　Campaign of 1814.

WOODFORD, ALEXANDER, Colonel.
　　Maria Theresa. ⎱ 𝔒𝔘.
　　St. George, 4th Class. ⎰

WYLIE, Sir JAMES, Bart. Councillor of State and
First Physician to the Emperor of Russia.
† Wladimir. 20 March, 1807.

YEO, Sir JAMES LUCAS, Captain R.N. K.C.B. Died
on the Coast of Africa, 1818.
† Comm. of St. Bento D'Avis. 16 March,
1810.
Reduction of Cayenne, 1808-9.
YORK, H. R. H. FREDERICK Duke of, K.G. Died
Jan. 1827.
Golden Fleece.
St. Esprit.
Maria Theresa.
Alexander Newski.
Red and White Eagle.
Charles III.

NOTE.

NOTE.

Since the foregoing List was printed, a further distribution of Foreign Orders has taken place among the Naval Officers engaged at the Battle of Navarino. Although, therefore, a few of them will be found in their alphabetical places, a complete List is here added.

Sir EDWARD CODRINGTON, Vice Admiral of the Blue, G.C.B.

    Grand Cross of St. Louis.

    St. George of Russia.

THOMAS FELLOWES, Captain R.N. C.B.

    Cross of Charles III.

    Comm. of the Legion of Honour.

    St. Anne, 2d Class.

JOHN A. OMMANEY, Captain R.N. C.B.

    Cross of St. Louis.

    St. Wladimir, 3d Class.

GAWEN W. HAMILTON, Captain R.N. C.B.

    Cross of St. Louis.

    St. Anne, 2d Class.

Hon. J. A. MAUDE, Captain R.N. C.B.

    Cross of St. Louis.

    St. Anne, 2d Class.

Hon. FREDERICK SPENCER, Captain R.N. C.B.
    Cross of St. Louis.
    St. Anne, 2d Class.
EDWARD CURZON, Captain R.N. C.B.
    Cross of St. Louis.
    St. Wladimir, 3d Class.
LEWIS DAVIES, Captain R.N. C.B.
    Cross of St. Louis.
    St. Anne, 2d Class.
Hon. WILLIAM ANSON, Captain R.N. C.B.
    Cross of St. Louis.
    St. Anne, 2d Class.
Rt. Hon. HENRY Viscount INGESTRIE, Captain R.N.
    C.B.
        Cross of St. Louis.
        St. Anne, 2d Class.
RICHARD DICKINSON, Commander R.N. C.B.
    Cross of St. Louis.
    St. Anne, 2d Class.
GEORGE B. MARTIN, Commander R.N. C.B.
    Cross of St. Louis.
    St. Anne, 2d Class.
HENRY JOHN CODRINGTON, Midshipman R.N.
    St. Wladimir, 4th Class.

K

KNIGHTS OF THE MOST NOBLE ORDER OF THE GARTER.

The number of Knights of this Order were limited by the Founder to twenty-six, including the Sovereign, and that number remained unaltered till 3 June, 1786, when a statute passed making the number twenty-six *exclusive of the Sons of the Sovereign or his successors*. Subsequent statutes have been passed to authorise the election of *Foreign Sovereigns* into the Order: and in one instance two English Knights (the Earl of Liverpool and Viscount Castlereagh) were, by especial statute, admitted into the Order; but no further elections took place until the number was again reduced to twenty-five.

At the Accession of King George the Third this Order consisted (one stall being then vacant) of

.THE SOVEREIGN, King GEORGE III.
>Died 29 Jan. 1820.

H. R. H. EDWARD AUGUSTUS Duke of YORK.
>Died 17 Sept. 1767.

H. R. H. WILLIAM Duke of CUMBERLAND.
>Died 31 Oct. 1765.

H. S. H. FREDERICK III. Duke of SAXE GOTHA.
Died 10 March, 1772.

H. S. H. WILLIAM GEORGE Landgrave of HESSE
CASSELL. Died 31 Oct. 1785.

H. S. H. WILLIAM V. Prince of ORANGE.
Died 9 April, 1806.

H. S. H. FERDINAND Duke of BRUNSWICK LUNEN-
BURG. Died 1788.

LIONEL Duke of DORSET. Died 10 Oct. 1763.

THOMAS Duke of NEWCASTLE. Died 17 Nov. 1768.

JOHN Duke of RUTLAND. Died 29 May, 1779.

PHILIP Earl of CHESTERFIELD. Died 24 March,
1773.

EVELYN Duke of KINGSTON. Died 23 Oct. 1773.

WILLIAM Duke of PORTLAND. Died 1 May, 1762.

THOMAS Duke of LEEDS. Died 23 March, 1789.

JOHN Duke of BEDFORD. Died 14 Jan. 1771.

JOHN Earl GRANVILLE. Died 2 Jan. 1763.

HENRY Earl of LINCOLN. Died 22 Feb. 1794.

DANIEL Earl of WINCHILSEA. Died 2 Aug. 1769.

GEORGE Earl of CARDIGAN. (Afterwards Duke of
Montagu.) Died 23 May, 1790.

WILLIAM Duke of DEVONSHIRE. Died 2 Oct. 1764.

HUGH Earl of NORTHUMBERLAND. Died 6 June,
1786.

FRANCIS Earl of HERTFORD. (Afterwards Marquess.)
Died 14 June, 1794.

JAMES Earl WALDEGRAVE. Died 8 April, 1763.

CHARLES Marquess of ROCKINGHAM. Died July, 1782.

RICHARD Earl TEMPLE. Died 11 Sept. 1779.

The only Installations of this Order, which have been celebrated with the usual ceremonies, in St. George's Chapel, during the reigns of King George III. or of His present MAJESTY, were on the 22 Sept. 1762, 25 July, 1771, and 23 April, 1805. Wherever, therefore, any other date of Installation occurs, it is to be understood that the Knight was installed by Dispensation, that is, that a Warrant had passed the Royal Sign Manual and Seal of the Order, permitting the said Knight elect to wear the Collar and to have his Banner, &c. placed in the Chapel, as though he had been personally installed.

Knights since the Accession of King George III.

ABERCORN, JOHN JAMES Marquess of.
Elected 17 Jan. 1805. Installed 23 April, 1805.
Died 27 Jan. 1818.

ALBEMARLE, GEORGE Earl of.
Elect. 26 Dec. 1765. Inst. 25 July, 1771.
Died 13 Aug. 1772,

ANGLESEY, HENRY WILLIAM Marquess of.
Inst. 2 March, 1818.

AUSTRIA, FRANCIS Emperor of.
Elect. 9 June, 1814. Inst. 27 Dec. 1814.

BATH, THOMAS Marquess of.
>Elect. 3 June, 1778.   Never installed.
>Died 19 Nov. 1796.

BATH, THOMAS Marquess of.
>Elect. 16 July, 1823.   Inst. 29 July, 1823.

BATHURST, HENRY Earl.
>Elect. 24 July, 1817.   Inst. 26 July, 1817.

BEAUFORT, HENRY Duke of.
>Elect. 2 June, 1786.   Inst. 29 May, 1801.
>Died 11 Oct. 1803.

BEAUFORT, HENRY CHARLES Duke of.
>Elect. 18 Jan. 1805.   Inst. 23 April, 1805.

BRUNSWICK, CHARLES WILLIAM FERDI-
NAND Duke of.
>Elect. 1766.   Inst. 25 July, 1771.
>Died 10 Nov. 1806, of wounds received at
>the Battle of Averstadt.

BUCCLEUGH, HENRY Duke of.
>Elect. 28 May, 1794.   Inst. 29 May, 1801.
>Died 11 Jan. 1812.

BUCKINGHAM, GEORGE Marquess of.
>Elect. 2 June, 1786.   Inst. 29 May, 1801.
>Died 11 Feb. 1813.

BUCKINGHAM and CHANDOS, RICHARD Duke of.
>Elect. 7 June, 1820.   Inst. 12 June, 1820.

BUTE, JOHN Earl of.
>Elect. 1762.   Inst. 22 Sept. 1762.
>Died 10 March, 1792.

CAMBRIDGE, H. R. H. ADOLPHUS FREDERICK.
>Elect. 2 June, 1786.   Inst. 28 May, 1801.

CAMDEN, JOHN Earl.
>Elect. 14 Aug. 1799.   Inst. 29 May, 1801.

CARLISLE, FREDERICK Earl of.
>Elect. 12 June, 1793.   Inst. 29 May, 1801.
>Died 4 Sept. 1825.

CHATHAM, JOHN Earl of.
>Elect. 15 Dec. 1790.   Inst. 29 May, 1801.

CHESTERFIELD, PHILIP Earl of.
>Elect. 18 Jan. 1805.   Inst. 23 April, 1805.
>Died 29 Aug. 1815.

CHOLMONDELEY, GEORGE JAMES Marquess.
>Elect. 22 June, 1822.   Inst. 22 July, 1822.
>Died 10 April, 1827.

CLARENCE, H. R. H. WILLIAM HENRY Duke of.
>Elect. 1782.   Inst. 28 May, 1801.

CORNWALLIS, CHARLES Marquess.
>Elect. 2 June, 1786.   Inst. 29 May, 1801.
>Died 5 Oct. 1805.

CUMBERLAND, H. R. H. HENRY FREDERICK Duke of.
>Elect. 21 Dec. 1767.   Inst. 25 July, 1771.
>Died 18 Sept. 1796.

CUMBERLAND, H. R. H. ERNEST AUGUSTUS Duke of.
 Elect. 2 June, 1786. Inst. 28 May, 1801.

DARTMOUTH, GEORGE Earl of.
 Elect. 27 May, 1805. Never installed.
 Died 4 Dec. 1810.
DENMARK, FREDERICK King of.
 Elect. 13 Feb. 1822. Inst. 22 July, 1822.
DEVONSHIRE, WILLIAM Duke of.
 Elect. 19 April, 1782. Inst. 29 May, 1801.
 Died 29 July, 1811.
DEVONSHIRE, WILLIAM SPENCER Duke of.
 Elect. 10 May, 1827. Inst. 10 May, 1827.
DORSET, JOHN FREDERICK Duke of.
 Elect. 9 April, 1788. Never installed.
 Died 19 July, 1799.
DORSET, CHARLES Duke of.
 Elect. 30 Jan. 1826. Inst. 30 Jan. 1826.

EXETER, BROWNLOW, Marquess of.
 Elect. 10 May, 1827. Inst. 10 May, 1827.

FRANCE, LOUIS XVIII. King of.
> Elect. 21 April, 1814. Inst. 21 April, 1814.
> Died 16 Sept. 1824.

FRANCE, CHARLES X. King of.
> Elect. 9 March, 1825. Inst. 20 Dec. 1825.

GLOUCESTER, H. R. H. WILLIAM HENRY Duke of.
> Elect. 27 May, 1762. Inst. 22 Sept. 1762.
> Died 25 Aug. 1805.

GLOUCESTER, H. R. H. WILLIAM FREDERICK Duke of.
> Elect. 16 July, 1794. Inst. 29 May, 1801.

GRAFTON, AUGUSTUS HENRY Duke of.
> Elect. 20 Sept. 1769. Inst. 25 July, 1771.
> Died 14 March, 1811.

HALIFAX, GEORGE Earl of.
> Elect. 1764.   Never installed.
> Died 1771.

HARDWICK, PHILIP Earl of.
> Elect. 3 Dec. 1803. Inst. 23 April, 1805.

HASTINGS, FRANCIS Marquess of.
> Elect. 12 June, 1812. Inst. 13 June, 1812.
> Died 28 Nov. 1826.

HERTFORD, FRANCIS Marquess of.
        Elect. 18 July, 1807. Inst. 31 March, 1812.
        Died 17 June, 1822.
HERTFORD, FRANCIS CHARLES Marquess of.
        Elect. 22 Nov. 1822. Inst. Nov. 1822.
HESSE CASSELL, H. S. H. WILLIAM Landgrave of.
        Elect. 1772. Inst. 19 May, 1801.
        Died 19 May, 1808.
HOWE, RICHARD Earl.
        Elect. 2 June, 1797.   Never installed.
        Died 5 Aug. 1799.

KENT, H. R. H. EDWARD Duke of.
        Elect. 2 June, 1786. Inst. 28 May, 1801.
        Died 23 Jan. 1820.

LANSDOWNE, WILLIAM Marquess of.
        Elect. 19 April, 1782.   Inst. 29 May, 1801.
        - Died 7 May, 1805.
LEEDS, FRANCIS GODOLPHIN Duke of.
        Elect. 15 Dec. 1790.   Never installed.
        Died 31 Jan. 1799.

LEEDS, GEORGE WILLIAM FREDERICK Duke of.
Elect. 10 May, 1827.   Inst. 10 May, 1827.
LIVERPOOL, ROBERT BANKS Earl of.
Elect. 9 June, 1814.   Inst. 28 June, 1814.
LONDONDERRY, ROBERT Marquess of.
Elect. 9 June, 1814.   Inst. 28 June, 1814.
Died 12 Aug. 1822.
LONSDALE, WILLIAM Earl of.
Elect. 18 July, 1807.   Inst. 31 March, 1812.

MARLBOROUGH, GEORGE Duke of.
Elect. 12 Dec. 1768.   Inst. 25 July, 1771.
Died 30 Jan. 1817.
MECKLENBURG STRELITZ, H. S. H. FREDE-
RICK IV. Duke of.
Elect. 23 April, 1764.   Inst. 25 July, 1771.
Died 2 June, 1794.
MONTROSE, JAMES Duke of.
Elect. 26 March, 1812.   Inst. 31 March,
1812.

NETHERLANDS, WILLIAM King of The.
>Elect. 1814.   Inst. 27 Dec. 1814.

NEWCASTLE, HENRY PELHAM Duke of.
>Elect. 19 June, 1812.   Inst. 22 June, 1812.

NORTHUMBERLAND, HUGH Duke of.
>Elect. 9 April, 1788.   Inst. 29 May, 1801.
>Died 10 July, 1817.

NORTHUMBERLAND, HUGH Duke of.
>Elect. 25 Nov. 1819.   Inst. 4 Dec. 1819.

PEMBROKE, GEORGE AUGUSTUS Earl of.
>Elect. 17 Jan. 1805.   Inst. 23 April, 1805.
>Died 24 Oct. 1827.

PORTLAND, WILLIAM HENRY Duke of.
>Elect. 16 July, 1794.   Inst. 29 May, 1801.
>Died 30 Oct. 1809.

PORTUGAL, JOHN VI. King of.
>Elect. 13 Feb. 1822.   Inst. 25 Nov. 1823.
>Died 10 March, 1826.

PRUSSIA, FREDERICK WILLIAM III. King of.
>Elect. 1814.   Inst. 19 June, 1814.

RICHMOND, CHARLES (Third) Duke of.
    Elect. 19 April, 1782.　Inst. 29 May, 1801.
    Died 29 Dec. 1806.

RICHMOND, CHARLES (Fourth) Duke of.
    Elect. 1812.　Inst. 31 March, 1812.
    Died 28 Aug. 1819.

ROCHFORD, WILLIAM HENRY Earl of.
    Elect. 3 June, 1778.　Never installed.
    Died 20 Sept. 1781.

ROXBURGH, JOHN Duke of.
    Elect. 3 June, 1801.　Inst. 3 June, 1801.
    Died 1804.

RUSSIA, ALEXANDER Emperor of.
    Elect. 27 July, 1813.　Inst. 19 April, 1814.
    Died 19 Nov. 1825.

RUSSIA, NICHOLAS Emperor of.
    Elect. 16 March, 1827.　Inst. 4 Sept. 1827.

RUTLAND, CHARLES Duke of.
    Elect. 3 Oct. 1782.　Never installed.
    Died 24 Oct. 1787.

RUTLAND, JOHN HENRY Duke of.
    Elect. 25 Nov. 1803.　Inst. 31 March, 1812.

SALISBURY, JAMES Marquess of.
    Elect. 12 June, 1793.　Inst. 29 May, 1801.
    Died 13 June, 1823.

SAXE COBOURG, LEOPOLD GEORGE FREDERICK Prince of.
> Elect. 23 May, 1816. Inst. 25 May, 1816.

SAXE GOTHA, H. S. H. ERNEST Duke of.
> Elect. 15 Dec. 1790. Inst. 19 May, 1801.
> Died 20 April, 1804.

SPAIN, FERDINAND VII. King of.
> Elect. 10 Aug. 1814. Inst. 26 Aug. 1815.

SPENCER, GEORGE JOHN Earl.
> Elect. 1 March, 1799. Inst. 29 May, 1801.

STAFFORD, GRANVILLE Marquess of.
> Elect. 11 Feb. 1771. Inst. 25 July, 1771.
> Died 25 Oct. 1803.

STAFFORD, GEORGE GRANVILLE Marquess of.
> Elect. 22 March, 1806. Inst. 31 March, 1812.

SUFFOLK, HENRY Earl of.
> Elect. 3 June, 1778. Never installed.
> Died 6 March, 1779.

SUSSEX, H. R. H. AUGUSTUS FREDERICK Duke of.
> Elect. 2 June, 1786. Inst. 28 May, 1801.

WALES, Prince of, (now GEORGE IIII.)
> Elect. 26 Dec. 1765. Inst. 25 July, 1771.

WESTMORLAND, JOHN Earl of.
> Elect. 12 June, 1793. Inst. 29 May, 1801.

WELLESLEY, RICHARD Marquess of.
       Elect. 3 March, 1810. Inst. 31 March, 1812.

WELLINGTON, ARTHUR Duke of.
       Elect. 4 March, 1813. Inst. 19 April, 1814.

WINCHELSEA, GEORGE Earl of.
       Elect. 17 Jan. 1805. Inst. 23 April, 1805. .
       Died 2 Aug. 1826.

YORK, H. R. H. FREDERICK Duke of.
       Elect. 1770. Inst. 30 July; 1771.
       Died 5 Jan. 1827.

KNIGHTS OF THE MOST ANCIENT AND MOST NOBLE ORDER OF THE THISTLE.

The number of Knights of this Order was fixed by the original statutes at Twelve, exclusive of the Sovereign, and no extra Knights appear to have been nominated until His present MAJESTY, on the occasion of His Coronation, was pleased to nominate four, *viz.* The Marquess of Queensbury, The Earls of Cassilis and Lauderdale, and Viscount Melville; and there are now four extra Knights, *viz.* The Earls of Warwick, Aboyne, Fife, and Moray.

In this Order there is no Installation, but the Knight is entitled to wear the full Habit of the Order from the moment of his investiture.

At the Accession of King George the Third this Order consisted, besides the Sovereign, (one Stall being vacant,) of

CHARLES Earl of PORTMORE. Died 5 July, 1785.

WILLIAM Marquess of LOTHIAN. Died 28 July, 1767.

JOHN Earl of BUTE. Resigned on receiving the Garter, 1762.

JOHN Earl of HYNDFORD. Died 19 July, 1767.

L

WILLIAM Earl of DUMFRIES. Died 27 July, 1768.

FRANCIS Earl BROOKE and Earl of WARWICK. Died 6 July, 1773.

JAMES Duke of ATHOLL. Died 8 Jan. 1764.

JAMES Earl of MORTON. Died 12 Oct. 1768.

JAMES Earl of MORAY. Died 5 July, 1767.

LIONEL Earl of DYSART. Died 1770.

JOHN Earl of ROTHES. Died 10 Dec. 1767.

Knights nominated since the Accession of King George III.

ABERDEEN, GEORGE Earl of.
Invested 16 March, 1808.

ABERGAVENNY, GEORGE Earl of.
Inv. 23 May, 1814.

ABOYNE, GEORGE Earl of.
Inv. 1827.

AILESBURY, THOMAS Earl of.
Inv. 29 Oct. 1786. Died 19 April, 1814.

AILESBURY, CHARLES Marquess of.
Inv. 1819.

ARGYLL, JOHN Duke of.
Inv. 7 Aug. 1765. Died 9 Nov. 1770.

ATHOLL, JOHN Duke of.
Inv. 1767. Died 5 Nov. 1774.

ATHOLL, JOHN Duke of.
Inv. 1799.

BUCCLEUGH, HENRY Duke of.

> Inv. 23 Dec. 1767. Resigned on being elected K.G. 1794.

BUCCLEUGH, CHARLES WILLIAM HENRY Duke of.

> Inv. 22 May, 1812. Died 20 April, 1819.

CARLISLE, FREDERICK Earl of.

> Inv. at Turin, 27 Feb. 1768. Resigned on being elected K.G. 1793.

CASSILIS, ARCHIBALD Earl of.

> Inv. 17 July, 1821.

CATHCART, CHARLES Lord.

> Inv. 1763. Died 14 Aug. 1776.

CATHCART, WILLIAM SCHAW Earl.

> Inv. 23 Nov. 1805.

CLARENCE, H. R. H. WILLIAM HENRY Duke of.

> Inv. 5 April, 1770.

EGLINTON, HUGH Earl of.

> Inv. 22 May, 1812. Died 15 Dec. 1819.

ERSKINE, THOMAS Lord.

> Inv. 1815. Died 17 Nov. 1823.

FIFE, JAMES Earl of.
        Inv. 3 Sept. 1827.

GALLOWAY, JOHN Earl of.
        Inv. 1 Nov. 1775.   Died 14 Nov. 1806.
GALLOWAY, GEORGE Earl of.
        Inv. 30 May, 1814.
GORDON, ALEXANDER Duke of.
        Inv. 11 Jan. 1775.   Died 17 June, 1827.

HAMILTON, DOUGLAS Duke of.
        Inv. 23 Dec. 1785.   Died 2 Aug. 1799.

LAUDERDALE, JAMES Earl of.
        Inv. 17 July, 1821.
LOTHIAN, WILLIAM Marquess of.
        Inv. 26 Oct. 1768.   Died 12 April, 1775.
LOTHIAN, WILLIAM JOHN Marquess of.
        Inv. 11 Oct. 1776.   Died 4 Jan. 1815.

LOTHIAN, WILLIAM Marquess of.
>Inv. 1819.   Died 27 April, 1824.

MANSFIELD, DAVID Earl of.
>Inv. 1768.   Died 1 Sept. 1796.

MELVILLE, ROBERT Viscount.
>Inv. 17 July, 1821.

MONTROSE, JAMES Duke of.
>Inv. 14 June, 1793.   Resigned on being elected K.G. 1812.

MORAY, FRANCIS Earl of.
>Inv. 3 Sept. 1827.

MORTON, GEORGE Earl of.
>Inv. 26 July, 1797.   Died 17 July, 1827.

NORTHINGTON, ROBERT Earl of.
>Inv. 18 Aug. 1773.   Died July, 1786.

POULETT, JOHN Earl.
>Inv. 30 May, 1794.   Died 14 Jan. 1819.

QUEENSBURY, WILLIAM Duke of.
        Inv. 1761.   Died 28 Dec. 1810.
QUEENSBURY, CHARLES Marquess of.
        Inv. 17 July, 1821.

ROSEBERRY, NEIL Earl of.
        Inv. 4 March, 1771.   Died 25 March, 1814.
ROXBURGH, JOHN Duke of.
        Inv. 28 Nov. 1768.   Died 19 March, 1804.
        His Grace was elected K.G. 1801, and by the espe-
    cial favour of His late Majesty was allowed to retain
    the Thistle, a mark of Royal favour which had never
    before been conferred on any subject since James
    Duke of Hamilton, in the reign of Queen Anne.

TWEEDDALE, GEORGE Marquess of.
        Inv. 1820.

WARWICK, RICHARD Earl of.
        Inv. 1820.

KNIGHTS OF THE MOST HONOURABLE MILITARY ORDER OF THE BATH.

Called previous to 2 Jan. 1815, " KNIGHTS COM-
PANIONS," and subsequently to that date,
" KNIGHTS GRAND CROSSES."

The number of Knights of this Order was limited by the original statutes to Thirty-eight, including the Sovereign. Extra
Knights were, however, occasionally nominated, the first instance
being in the case of Sir George Murray Keith, Ambassador at
Copenhagen in 1772. In 1812 eleven extra Knights were nominated by an especial statute, and by a notification in the London
Gazette, 2 Jan. 1815, the Order was still further extended, and
divided into Three Classes, *viz.*

Knights GRAND CROSSES—Seventy-two, exclusive of the Sovereign and Princes of the Blood Royal.

Knights COMMANDERS—180, with power to the Sovereign to
add thereto.

COMPANIONS—Number unlimited.

A List of this latter Class (as the Companions, though form-
ing part of an Order of Knighthood, have not the rank of
Knights) does not come within the plan of this work.

At the Accession of King George the Third this Order
consisted (besides the SOVEREIGN) of

H. R. H. WILLIAM Duke of CUMBERLAND. Died
31 Oct. 1765.

GEORGE Earl CHOLMONDELEY. Died 10 June, 1770.

JOHN Earl DE LA WARR.   Died 16 March, 1766.

JOHN Earl of BREADALBANE.   Died 26 Jan. 1782.

Sir WILLIAM STANHOPE.   Died 1772.

Sir ROBERT CLIFTON, Bart.   Died 5 Dec. 1762.

WILLIAM Earl of INCHIQUIN.   Died July, 1777.

HENRY Duke of CHANDOS.   Died 28 Nov. 1771.

THOMAS Lord GRANTHAM.   Died 30 Sept. 1770.

JOHN Viscount LIGONIER.   Died 28 April, 1770.

RICHARD Viscount FITZWILLIAM, (of Ireland.)   Died
      25 May, 1776.

Sir THOMAS WHITMORE.   Died 15 April, 1773.

Sir HENRY CALTHORPE.   Died 14 April, 1788.

Sir W. MORTON HARBORD.   Died 17 Feb. 1770.

Sir EDWARD HAWKE, (afterwards LORD HAWKE.)
      Died 16 Oct. 1781.

Sir CHARLES HOWARD.   Died 26 Aug. 1765.

Sir JOHN MORDAUNT.   Died 23 Oct. 1780.

JOHN Lord POLLINGTON, (afterwards Earl of MEX-
      BOROUGH.)   Died 27 Feb. 1778.

RICHARD Lord ONSLOW.   Died 8 Oct. 1776.

Sir EDWARD WALPOLE.   Died 12 Jan. 1784.

CHARLES Duke of BOLTON.   Died 5 July, 1765.

Sir RICHARD LYTTELTON.   Died 1 Oct. 1770.

Sir EDWARD MONTAGU, (afterwards Earl BEAULIEU.)
      Died 25 Nov. 1802.

Sir WILLIAM ROWLEY.   Died 1 Jan. 1768.

WILLIAM Lord BLAKENEY.   Died 20 Sept. 1761.

JOHN Lord CARYSFORT.   Died Aug. 1772.

Sir JOSEPH YORKE, (afterwards Lord Dover.)   Died
    2 Dec. 1792.

Sir JAMES GRAY. Bart.   Died 9 Jan. 1773.

Sir WILLIAM BEAUCHAMP PROCTOR, Bart.   Died
    16 Sept. 1773.

Sir JOHN GIBBONS, Bart.   Died 1776.

Sir GEORGE POCOCK.   Died 3 April, 1792.

Sir GEFFRY AMHERST, (afterwards LORD AMHERST.)
    Died 3 Aug. 1797.

Sir JOHN GRIFFIN GRIFFIN, (afterwards Lord
    HOWARD DE WALDEN.)   Died 25 May, 1797.

Sir FRANCIS BLAKE DELAVAL.   Died 6 Aug. 1771.

Sir CHARLES FREDERICK.   Died 1786.

Sir GEORGE WARREN.   Died 30 Aug. 1801.

Sir CHARLES SAUNDERS.   Died 7 Dec. 1775.

NOTE.—The Installations of Knights of this Order (since
1760) have been .. 26 May, 1761
                    15 June, 1772
                    19 May, 1779
                    19 May, 1788
                    19 May, 1803
                    1 June, 1812.
Since the extension of the Order in 1815, no actual installation has taken place, and probably none will in future, the
Chapel being too small to admit of it; but Warrants of Dispensation are from time to time issued; wherever, therefore, in the
following List any other date of installation occurs than the
foregoing, it is to be understood as having been by Dispensation.

ABERCROMBIE, Sir RALPH:
        Invested 22 July, 1795.   Never installed.
        Killed in Egypt, 1801.

ABERCROMBIE, Sir ROBERT.
> Inv. 15 Aug. 1792.   Inst. 1803.
> Died Nov. 1827.

ABERCROMBY, Hon. Sir JOHN, (late K.C.B.)
> Nominated 7 April, 1815.
> Died 14 Feb. 1817.

ALTEN, CHARLES Count, (honorary.)
> Nom. 12 Aug. 1820.   Inst. 6 July, 1821.

AMHERST, JEFERY Baron.
> Inst. by Proxy, 26 May, 1761, and invested
> in the Camp at State Island, North Ame-
> rica, 25 Oct. following.
> Died 3 Aug. 1797.

ANGLESEY, The Most Hon. HENRY WILLIAM Marquess of, K.G. &c.
> Nom. 2 Jan. 1815.   Inst. 1821.

ANTRIM, The Most Hon. WILLIAM RANDALL Marquess of.
> Inv. 5 May, 1779.   Inst. 1779.
> Died 25 July, 1791.

AUCHMUTY, Sir SAMUEL.
> Nom. 22 Feb. 1812.   Inst. 1812.
> Died 11 Aug. 1822.

BAGOT, The Right Hon. Sir CHARLES.

    Inv. 27 May, 1820.   Inst. 1820.

BAIRD, Sir DAVID, Bart.

    Nom. 26 April, 1809.   Inst. 1812.

BANKS, Sir JOSEPH.

    Inv. 1 July, 1795.   Inst. 1803.

    Died 19 June, 1820.

BARCLAY DE TOLLY, Count, (honorary.)

    Nom. 9 Sept. 1815.

    Died May, 1818.

BARLOW, Sir GEORGE HILARO, Bart.

    Nom. 29 Oct. 1806.   Inst. 1812.

BECKWITH, Sir GEORGE.

    Nom. 26 April, 1809.   Inst. 1812.

    Died 20 March, 1823.

BELLAMONT, The Right Hon. CHARLES Earl of.

    Inv. at Dublin Castle 16 Jan. 1764.   Inst.

      1772.

    Died 20 Oct. 1806.

BENTINCK, The Right Hon. Lord WILLIAM.

    Nom. 29 Jan. 1813.   Inst. 1821.

BERESFORD, The Rt. Hon. WILLIAM CARR, Viscount.

    Nom. 23 Oct. 1810.   Inst. 1812.

BERKELEY, Hon. Sir GEORGE CRANFIELD.

    Inv. 4 March, 1813.

    Died 25 Feb. 1818.

BLAQUIERE, Right Hon. JOHN Baron DE.

    Inv. 3 Aug. 1774.   Inst. 1779.

    Died 27 Aug. 1812.

BLIGH, Sir RICHARD RODNEY.
> Nom. 27 May, 1820.
> Died 30 April, 1821.

BLOMEFIELD, Right Hon. BENJAMIN Baron.
> Inv. 1 April, 1822.

BLUCHER, Prince, (honorary.)
> Nom. 9 Sept. 1815.
> Died 10 Sept. 1819.

BOYD, Sir ROBERT.
> Nom. 28 Jan. 1785.   Inst. 1788.
> Died in May, 1794.

BROWNRIGG, Sir ROBERT, Bart.
> Nom. 2 Jan. 1815.   Inst. 1821.

BRIDPORT, Right Hon. ALEXANDER Viscount.
> Inv. 7 May, 1788.   Inst. 1788.
> Died 3 May, 1814.

CALDWELL, Sir BENJAMIN.
> Nom. 27 May, 1820.
> Died Nov. 1820.

CALVERT, Sir HENRY, Bart.
> Nom. 2 Jan. 1815.   Inst. 1821.
> Died 4 Sept. 1826.

CAMBRIDGE, H. R. H. ADOLPHUS FREDERICK Duke of, K.G. &c.
> Nov. 2 Jan. 1815.   Inst. 1821.

CAMPBELL, Sir ARCHIBALD.
>> Inv. 30 Sept. 1785.   Inst. 1788.
>> Died 31 March, 1791.

CAMPBELL, Sir ARCHIBALD.   (Late K.C.B.)
>> Nom. 26 Dec. 1826.

CAMPBELL, Sir GEORGE.
>> Nom. 1820.
>> Died 23 Jan. 1821.

CARYSFORT, Right Hon. JOHN Earl of.
>> Inv. 23 March, 1761.   Inst. 1761.
>> Died 18 Oct. 1772.

CATHERLOUGH, Right Hon. ROBERT Earl of.
>> Inv. 18 May, 1770.   Never installed.
>> Died 30 March, 1772.

CHRISTIAN, Sir HUGH CLOBERY.
>> Inv. 17 Feb. 1796.   Never installed.
>> Died Nov. 1798.

CLANCARTY, Right Hon. RICHARD LE POER Earl of
>> (Marquess of Heusden, &c.)
>> Nom. 1 April, 1815.   Inst. 1821.

CLARENCE, H. R. H. WILLIAM HENRY Duke of,
>> K.G. &c.
>> Nom. 2 Jan. 1815.   Inst. 1821.

CLARKE, Sir ALURED.
>> Nom. 14 Jan. 1797.   Inst. 1803.

CLAVERING, Sir JOHN.
>> Nom. 8 Nov. 1777.   Never installed.
>> Died in India, 10 April, 1778.

CLINTON, Sir HENRY.
>> Inv. 11 April, 1777.   Inst. 1779.
>> Died 23 Dec. 1795.

CLINTON, Sir HENRY.
>> Inv. 28 July, 1814.   Inst. 1821.

CLINTON, Sir WILLIAM HENRY.
>> Nom. 2 Jan. 1815.   Inst. 1821.

CLIVE, The Right Hon. ROBERT Lord.
>> Inv. 24 April, 1764.   Inst. 1772.
>> Died 22 Nov. 1774.

COCHRANE, Sir THOMAS, (commonly called the Right Hon. Lord COCHRANE.)
>> Inv. 26 April, 1809.   Inst. 1812.
>> Degraded 1815.

COCHRANE, The Hon. Sir ALEXANDER-FORESTER, Admiral of the White.
>> Nom. 29 March, 1806.   Inst. 1812.

COCKBURN, Sir GEORGE, Vice Admiral of the White.
>> Nom. 20 Feb. 1818.   Inst. 1821.

CODRINGTON, Sir EDWARD, Vice Admiral of the Red.
>> Nom. 13 Nov. 1827.

COLE, Hon. Sir GALBRAITH LOWRY.
>> Nom. 29 Jan. 1813.   Inst. 1821.

COLPOYS, Sir JOHN.
>> Inv. 14 Feb. 1798.   Inst. 1803.

COLVILLE, Hon. Sir CHARLES.
>> Nom. 7 April, 1815.   Inst. 1821.

COMBERMERE, The Right Hon. STAPLETON Lord.
   .Nom. 21 Aug. 1812. Inst. 1821.

COOTE, Sir EYRE.
   Inv. 30 Aug. 1771. Inst. 1772.
   Died 26 April, 1783.

COOTE, Sir EYRE.
   Inv. 19 May, 1802. Inst. 1803.
   Degraded 1816.

CORNWALLIS, The Hon. Sir WILLIAM.
   Nom. 2 Jan. 1815.
   Died 5 July, 1819.

COWLEY, The Right Hon. HENRY Lord.
   Nom. and inst. 1812.

CRAIG, Sir JAMES HENRY.
   Nom. 14 Jan. 1797. Inst. 1803.
   Died 12 Jan. 1812.

CUMBERLAND, H. R. H. ERNEST AUGUSTUS Duke
  of, K.G. &c.
   Nom. 2 Jan. 1815. Inst. 1821.

CURTIS, Sir ROGER, Bart.
   Nom. 2 Jan. 1815.
   Died 14 Nov. 1816.

CRAUFURD, Sir CHARLES GREGAN.
   Nom. 27 May, 1820.
   Died April, 1821.

DALHOUSIE, The Right Hon. GEORGE Earl of.

> Nom. 11 Sept. 1813.   Inst. 1821.

DELAVAL, Sir FRANCIS BLAKE.

> Inv. 23 March, 1761.   Inst. 1761.
>
> Died 6 Aug. 1771.

DOMETT, Sir WILLIAM, Ad. of the White, (late K.C.B.)

> Nom. 16 May, 1820.   Inst. 1821.

DON, Sir GEORGE.

> Nom. 27 May, 1820.   Inst. 1821.

DONOUGHMORE, The Right Hon. JOHN HENRY Earl of.

> Nom. 30 May, 1801.   Inst. 1803.

DORCHESTER, The Right Hon. GUY Lord.

> Nom. 6 July, 1776.   Inst. 1779.
>
> > He had a warrant to invest himself, being then Governor of Quebec and Commander of the Forces in Canada.
>
> Died 10 Nov. 1808.

DOVER, The Right Hon. JOSEPH Lord.

> Inv. 30 March, 1761.   Inst. 1761.
>
> Died 2 Dec. 1792.

DOYLE, Sir JOHN.

> Inv. 1 Feb. 1813.   Inst. 1821.

DRAPER, Sir WILLIAM.

> Inv. 27 Dec. 1765.   Inst. 1772.
>
> Died in 1788.

DRUMMOND, Sir GORDON.

> Nom. 7 Jan. 1817.   Inst. 1821.

DUCKWORTH, Sir JOHN THOMAS.

> Nom. 6 June, 1801.   Inst. 1803.
>
> Died 31 Aug. 1817.

DUNDAS, Sir DAVID.
>Inv. 28 April, 1803. Inst. 1803.
>Died 18 Feb. 1820.

EXMOUTH, The Right Hon. EDWARD Viscount, Admiral of the White. (Late K.C.B.)
>Nom. 16 March, 1816. Inst. 1821.

FANE, Sir HENRY.
>Nom. 24 Jan. 1826.

FARNBOROUGH, The Right Hon. CHARLES Lord.
>Nom. 27 May, 1820. Inst. 1821.

FAWCETT, Sir WILLIAM.
>Inv. 20 Dec. 1786. Inst. 1788.
>Died 22 March, 1804.

FOLEY, Sir THOMAS.
>Nom. 16 May, 1820. Inst. 1821.

FRANCIS, Sir PHILIP.
>Inv. 29 Oct. 1806. Inst. 1812.
>Died 22 Dec. 1818.

FREDERICK, Sir CHARLES.
>Inv. 23 March, 1761. Inst. 1761.
>Died 18 Dec. 1785.

M

FREMANTLE, Sir THOMAS FRANCIS.
>   Nom. 20 Feb. 1818.
>   Died 19 Dec. 1819.

FRIMONT, Baron. (Honorary.)
>   Nom. 17 April, 1819.   Inst. 1821.

GALWAY, The Right Hon. ROBERT Viscount.
>   Inv. 20 Dec. 1786.   Inst. 1788.
>   Died 23 July, 1810.

GAMBIER, The Right Hon. JAMES Lord, Admiral of
    the Red.
>   Nom. 7 June, 1815.   Inst. 1821.

GIBBONS, Sir JOHN, Bart.
>   Inv. 23 March, 1761.   Inst. 1761.
>   Died 9 July, 1776.

GLOUCESTER, H. R. H. WILLIAM FREDERICK Duke
    of, K.G. &c.
>   Nom. 2 Jan. 1815.   Inst. 1821.

GORDON, The Most Noble GEORGE Duke of.
>   Inv. 27 May, 1820.   Inst. 1821.

GORDON, Sir WILLIAM.
>   Inv. 3 Feb. 1775.   Inst. 1779.
>   Died 26 Jan. 1798.

GRANVILLE, The Right Hon. GRANVILLE Viscount.
>   Inv. at the Thuilleries, by the King of France,
>   9 June, 1825.

GRAVES, Sir THOMAS.
> Nom. 19 May, 1801.   Inst. 1803.
> Died 1814.

GRAY, Sir JAMES, Bart.
> Inv. at Naples, 23 Jan. 1761.   Inst. by
> Proxy, 1761.
> Died 9 Jan. 1773.

GREY, The Right Hon. CHARLES Earl.
> Nom. 1782.   Inst. 1788.
> Died 14 Nov. 1807.

GUNNING, Sir ROBERT, Bart.
> Inv. at Petersburgh, June, 1773.   Inst. 1779.
> Died 22 Sept. 1816.

HALDIMAND, Sir FREDERICK.
> Inv. 30 Sept. 1785.   Inst. 1788.
> Died 5 June, 1801.

HAMILTON, Sir WILLIAM.
> Inv. 15 Jan. 1772.   Inst. 1772.
> Died 6 April, 1813.

HARCOURT, The Right Hon. WILLIAM Earl of.
> Inst. 27 May, 1820.   Inst. 1821.

HARRIS, The Right Hon. GEORGE Lord.
> Inv. 27 May, 1820.   Inst. 1821.

HARVEY, Sir ELIAB, Adm. of the Blue, (late K.C.B.)
> Nom. 11 Jan. 1825.

HARVEY, Sir HENRY.

       Inv. 8 Jan. 1800. Inst. 1803.

       Died 28 Dec. 1810.

HASTINGS, The Most Hon. FRANCIS Marquess of.

       Nom. 14 Oct. 1818. Inst. 1821.

       Died 28 Nov. 1826.

HEATHFIELD, The Right Hon. GEORGE AUGUSTUS Lord.

       Nom. 1783. Inst. 1788.

       Died 6 July, 1790.

HENLEY, The Right Hon. MORTON Lord.

       Inv. at Berlin, 1 Jan. 1792. Inst. 1803.

HEYTESBURY, The Right Hon. WILLIAM Lord.

       Nom. 20 Sept. 1819. Inst. 6 July, 1821.

HILL, The Right Hon. ROWLAND Lord.

       Nom. 22 Feb. 1812. Inst. 1812.

HISLOP, Sir THOMAS, Bart.

       Nom. 14 Oct. 1818. Inst. 1821.

HOOD, Sir SAMUEL, Bart.

       Nom. 26 Sept. 1804. Inst. 1812.

       Died 24 Dec. 1814.

HOOD, The Right Hon. SAMUEL Viscount.

       Nom. 2 Jan. 1815.

       Died 27 Jan. 1816.

HOPE, Sir ALEXANDER.

       Inv. 29 June, 1813. Inst. 1821.

HOPE, Sir WILLIAM JOHNSTONE.

       Nom. 4 Oct. 1825.

HOPETOUN, The Right Hon. JOHN Earl of.
    Inv. 26 April, 1809.   Inst. 1812.
    Died 27 Aug. 1823.

HOTHAM, Sir CHARLES, Bart.
    Inv. 15 May, 1772.   Inst. 1772.
    Died 25 Jan. 1794.

HOWARD, Sir GEORGE.
    Inv. 3 Aug. 1774.   Inst. 1779.
    Died 16 July, 1796.

HOWARD OF EFFINGHAM, The Right Hon. KENNETH
    ALEXANDER Lord, (late K.C.B.)
    Nom. 17 March, 1820.   Inst. 1821.

HOWARD OF WALDEN, The Right Hon. JOHN Lord.
    Inv. 23 March, 1761.   Inst. 1761.
    Died 25 May, 1797.

HOWDEN, The Right Hon. JOHN FRANCIS Lord.
    Inv. 16 Feb. 1803.   Inst. 1803.

HOWE, The Right Hon. WILLIAM Viscount.
    Nom. Oct. 1776.   Inst. 1779.
    Died 5 Aug. 1799.

HUGHES, Sir EDWARD.
    Inv. 9 Dec. 1778.   Inst. 1779.
    Died 17 Jan. 1794.

IRWIN, Sir JOHN.
> Inv. 15 Dec. 1775.   Inst. 1779.
> Died June, 1788.

JOHNSON, Sir HENRY, Bart.
> Inv. 27 May, 1820.   Inst. 1821.

KEATS, Sir RICHARD GOODWIN, Admiral of the Blue.
> Inv. 12 July, 1809.   Inst. 1812.

KEITH, Sir ROBERT MURRAY.
> Nom. 29 Feb. 1772.   Inst. by Proxy, 1772.
> Died 1795.
>> NOTE.—Sir Robert's nomination was the first instance of a supernumerary Knight being added to the Order.

KEITH, The Right Hon. GEORGE Viscount.
> Inv. 30 May, 1794.   Inst. 1803.
> Died 1823.

KEMPT, Sir JAMES.
> Nom. 9 Sept. 1815.   Inst. 1821.

KENT, H. R. H. EDWARD Duke of.
> Nom. 2 Jan. 1815.
> Died 23 Jan. 1820.

KEPPELL, Sir WILLIAM.
> Inv. 1 Feb. 1813.   Inst. 1821.

KNOWLES, Sir CHARLES HENRY, Bart. Admiral of
the Red.
> Nom. 20 May, 1820.   Inst. 1821.

LAVINGTON, The Right Hon. RALPH Lord.
   Inv. 18 Feb. 1771. Inst. by Proxy, 1772.
   Died 1 Aug. 1807.
LEITH, Sir JAMES.
   Inv. 4 March, 1813.
   Died 16 Oct. 1816.
LIGONIER, The Right Hon. EDWARD Earl.
   Nom. 1781. Never installed.
   Died 14 June, 1782.
LINDSAY, Sir JOHN.
   Invested by the Nabob of Arcot, 11 March,
    1771. Inst. 1772.
   Died June, 1788.
LISTON, The Right Hon. Sir ROBERT.
   Inv. 21 Oct. 1816. Inst. 1821.
LONDONDERRY, The Most Hon. CHARLES WILLIAM
 Marquess of.
   Nom. 1 Feb. 1813. Inst. 1821.
LUDLOW, The Right Hon. GEORGE JAMES Earl.
   Inv. 14 Nov. 1804. Inst. 1812.
LYNCH, Sir WILLIAM.
   Inv. at Turin, 11 March, 1771. Inst. 1772.
   Died 25 Aug. 1785.
LYNEDOCH, The Right Hon. THOMAS Lord.
   Nom. 22 Feb. 1812. Inst. 1812.

MACARTNEY, The Right Hon. GEORGE Earl.
>Inv. in Dublin.   Inst. by Proxy, 1772.
>Died 31 March, 1806.

MAITLAND, The Hon. Sir THOMAS.
>Nom. 2 Jan. 1815.   Inst. 1821.
>Died 17 Jan. 1824.

MALCOLM, Sir JOHN.
>Nom. 26 Nov. 1819.   Inst. 1821.

MALMESBURY, The Right Hon. JAMES Earl of.
>Inv. at St. Petersburgh, 26 March, 1779.
>Inst. 1779.   Died 21 Nov. 1820.

MANN, Sir HORATIO, Bart.
>Inv. at Florence, 25 Oct. 1768.   Inst. by
>Proxy, 1772.
>Died 6 Nov. 1786.

MARTIN, Sir GEORGE, (late K.C.B.)
>Nom. 23 Feb. 1821.   Inst. 1821.

MEDOWS, Sir WILLIAM.
>Inv. 14 Dec. 1792.   Inst. 1803.
>Died 1813.

MITCHELL, Sir ANDREW.
>Inv. 13 Dec. 1765.   Never installed.
>Died 28 Jan. 1771.

MITCHELL, Sir ANDREW.
>Inv. 8 Jan. 1800.   Inst. 1803.
>Died 26 Feb. 1806.

MONTAGU, Sir GEORGE, Admiral of the Red.
      Nom. 2 Jan. 1815.   Inst. 1821.

MONTAGUE, Sir CHARLES.
      Inv. 18 Feb. 1771.   Inst. 1772.
      Died 1 Aug. 1777.

MOORE, Sir JOHN, Bart.
      Inv. 18 May, 1770.   Inst. by Proxy, 1772.
      Died 2 Feb. 1779.

MOORE, Sir JOHN.
      Inv. 14 Nov. 1804.   Never installed.
      Slain at Corunna, 1809.

MULGRAVE, The Right Hon. HENRY Earl of.
      Inv. 27 May, 1820.   Inst. 1821.

MUNRO, Sir HECTOR.
      Inv. by the Nabob of Arcot, 1778.   Inst 1779.
      Died 1806.

MURRAY, Sir GEORGE.
      Nom. 11 Sept. 1813.   Inst. 1821.

NEALE, Sir HARRY, Bart.
      Nom. 14 Sept. 1822.

NELSON, The Right Hon. HORATIO Viscount.
      Inv. 27 Sept. 1797.   Inst. 1803.
      Slain at Trafalgar, 1805.

NORTHESK, The Right Hon. WILLIAM Earl of.
      Inv. 5 June, 1806.   Inst. 1812.

NUGENT, Sir GEORGE, Bart.
Nom. 1 Feb. 1813. Inst. 1821.

OAKES, Sir HILDEBRAND, Bart.
Inv. 27 May, 1820. Inst. 1821.
Died 9 Sept. 1822.

OCHTERLONY, Sir DAVID, Bart.
Nom. 10 Dec. 1816. Inst. 1821.
Died 15 July, 1825.

ONSLOW, Sir RICHARD, Bart.
Nom. 2 Jan. 1815.
Died 27 Dec. 1817.

ORANGE, H. R. H. WILLIAM Prince of.
Inv. at Brussells, 16 Aug. 1814.

OSWALD, Sir JOHN, (late K.C.B.)
Nom. 25 Feb. 1824.

OUGHTON, Sir JAMES ADOLPHUS.
Inv. 22 Feb. 1773. Inst. 1779.
Died 13 April, 1780.

PAGET, Right Hon. Sir ARTHUR.
Nom. 26 May, 1804. Inst. 1812.

PAGET, Hon. Sir EDWARD.
      Nom. 12 June, 1812.   Inst. 1821.

PAKENHAM, Sir EDWARD MICHAEL. .
      Nom. 11 Feb. 1813.
      Killed at New Orleans 8 Jan. 1815.

PAKENHAM, Hon. Sir THOMAS.
      Inv. 27 May, 1820.   Inst. 1821.

PEIRSON, Sir RICHARD.
      Nom. 13 Nov. 1780.
      Died 13 Feb. 1781.

PICTON, Sir THOMAS.
      Inv. 1 Feb. 1813.   Never installed.
      Slain at Waterloo.

PITT, Hon. Sir WILLIAM AUGUSTUS.
      Inv. 15 Aug. 1792.   Inst. 1803.
      Died 29 Dec. 1809.

POCOCK, Sir GEORGE.
      Inv. 6 May, 1761.   Inst. 1761.
      Died 3 April, 1792.

POLE, Sir CHARLES MORICE, Bart.
      Nom. 20 Feb. 1818.   Inst. 1821.

PROCTOR, Sir WILLIAM BEAUCHAMP, Bart.
      Inv. 23 March, 1761.   Inst. 1761.
      Died 16 Sept. 1773.

RADSTOCK, The Right Hon. WILLIAM Lord.
      Nom. 2 Jan. 1815.   Inst. 1821.
      Died 20 Aug. 1825.

RODNEY, The Right Hon. GEORGE BRYDGES Lord.
> Nom. 1781. Inst. 1788.
> Died 21 May, 1792.

ROSSLYN, The Right Hon. JAMES Earl of.
> Nom. 27 May, 1820. Inst. 1821.

ST. VINCENT, The Right Hon. JOHN Earl of.
> Nom. 29 May, 1782. Inst. 1788.
> Died 15 March, 1823.

SAUMAREZ, Sir JAMES, Bart. Admiral of the White.
> Nom. 5 Sept. 1801. Inst. 1803.

SAUNDERS, Sir CHARLES.
> Inv. at Gibraltar, 6 July, 1761, having been
> previously installed by Proxy, 26 May,
> 1761.
> Died 7 Dec. 1775.

SAXE COBOURG, H. R. H. LEOPOLD Prince of.
> Inv. 23 May, 1816. Inst. 1821.

SCHWARTZENBERG, Prince, (honorary.)
> Nom. 9 Sept. 1815.
> Died Oct. 1820.

SHERBROOKE, Sir JOHN COPE.
> Nom. 16 Sept. 1809. Inst. 1812.

SLOPER, Sir ROBERT.
> Inv. 6 June, 1788. Never installed.
> Died Aug. 1802.

SPENCER, Sir BRENT.
>   Inv. 26 April, 1809.   Inst. 1812.

STEWART, Sir WILLIAM.
>   Nom. 11 Sept. 1813.   Inst. 1821.
>   Died 7 Jan. 1827.

STRACHAN, Sir RICHARD JOHN, Adm. of the Blue.
>   Inv. 4 March, 1807.   Inst. 1812.
>   Died 3 Feb. 1828.

STRANGFORD, The Right Hon. PERCY CLINTON SYD-
NEY Viscount.
>   Inv. 16 March, 1808.   Inst. 1812.

STUART, The Right Hon. Sir CHARLES.
>   Inv. 8 Jan. 1800.   Never installed.
>   Died 25 March, 1801.

STUART, Right Hon. Sir CHARLES.
>   Inv. 26 Sept. 1812.   Inst. 1815.

STUART, Sir JOHN, (Count of Maida.)
>   Inv. 4 March, 1807.   Inst. 1812.
>   Died 1815.

TARLETON, Sir BANASTRE, Bart.
>   Inv. 20 May, 1820.   Inst. 1821.

THOMPSON, Sir THOMAS BOULDEN, Bart. Vice Admiral of the Red, late K.C.B.
>   Nom. 14 Sept. 1822.
>   Died 3 March, 1828.

THORNBOROUGH, Sir EDWARD, Admiral of the White,
(late K.C.B.)
Nom. 11 Jan. 1825.

THORNTON, The Right Hon. Sir EDWARD.
Nom. 1821.

TRIGGE, Sir THOMAS.
Nom. 6 June, 1801.   Inst. 1803.
Died 11 Jan. 1814.

VAUGHAN, Hon. Sir JOHN.
Inv. 15 April, 1792.   Never installed.
Died 30 June, 1795.

VOLKONSKY, Prince, (honorary.)
Nom. 17 April, 1819.   Inst. 1821.

WALKER, Sir GEORGE TOWNSHEND, (late K.C.B.)
Inv. 21 April, 1817.   Inst. 1821.

WARREN, Sir GEORGE.
Inv. 25 March, 1761.   Inst. 1761.
Died 30 Aug. 1801.

WARREN, Sir JOHN BORLASE, Bart.
Inv. 30 May, 1794.   Inst. 1803.
Died 1822.

WELLESLEY, The Right Hon. Sir HENRY.   (See
    COWLEY, Lord.)
WELLINGTON, The Most Noble ARTHUR Duke of,
    &c. &c.
        Nom. 2 Aug. 1804.   Inst. 1812.
WHITWORTH, The Right Hon. CHARLES Earl.
        Inv. at St. Petersburgh, 17 Nov. 1793.
        Inst. 1803.
        Died 13 May, 1825.
WILLIAMSON, Sir ADAM.
        Inv. 18 Nov. 1794.   Never installed.
        Died Oct. 1798.
WORONZOW, Count, (honorary.)
        Nom. 17 April, 1819.   Inst. 1821.
WROUGHTON, Sir THOMAS.
        Nom. 13 Nov. 1780.   Never installed.
        Died 22 Aug. 1787.
WREDE, Prince, (honorary.)
        Nom. 9 Sept. 1815.   Inst. 1821.
WURTEMBURG, WILLIAM King of.
        Nom. 9 Sept. 1815.   Inst. 1821.

YONGE, Sir GEORGE, Bart.
        Inv. 7 May, 1788.   Inst. 1788.
        Died about 1810.

York, H. R. H. Frederick Duke of, K.G. &c. &c.
>   Inv. 30 Dec. 1768.   Inst. 1772.
>   Died 5 Jan. 1827.

Young, Sir William, Vice Admiral of England.
>   Nom. 12 July, 1814.
>   Died 25 Oct. 1821.

Zieten, Count, (honorary.)
>   Nom. 17 April, 1819.   Inst. 1821.

ORDER OF THE BATH.

KNIGHTS COMMANDERS.

*ABERCROMBY, Hon. Sir JOHN.
> Nominated G.C.B. 1815.
> Died 14 Feb. 1817.

*ACLAND, Sir WROTH PALMER, Lieutenant General.
> Died 8 March, 1816.

ADAM, Sir FREDERICK, Maj. Gen. K.M.T.—K.S.A.
> 16 Sept. 1818.

*ALAVA, Lieutenant General DON MIGUEL, (honorary.)

*ALTEN, CHARLES Count, Major General, (honorary.)
> Nom. G.C.

*ANSON, Sir GEORGE, Lieutenant General, C.T.S.

*ANSON, Sir WILLIAM, Lieutenant General.

*ARBUTHNOT, Sir ROBERT, Colonel, C.T.S.

*ARBUTHNOT, Sir THOMAS, Major General.

*ARENTSCHILDT, Colonel F. Baron de, (honorary.)

ARNOLD, Sir JOHN, Major General.

*AYLMER, MATHEW Lord, Lieutenant General.

*BARCLAY, Sir ROBERT, Major General, E.I.C.S.

BARLOW, Sir ROBERT, Knight, Rear Admiral.   20 May, 1826.

*BARNARD, Sir ANDREW F., now Major General, K.M.T. K.S.G. and K.C.H.

*BARNES, Sir EDWARD, Lieutenant General, K.M.T. K.S.A.

*BAYNTUN, Sir HENRY WILLIAM, Vice Admiral of the White.

*BEAUCLERK, Lord AMELIUS, Vice Admiral of the Red.

*BECKWITH, Sir THOMAS SYDNEY, Major General, C.T.S.

*BELL, Sir HENRY, Lieutenant General Royal Marines.

*BELSON, Sir CHARLES PHILIP, Major General.

BERESFORD, Sir JOHN Poo, Bart. Vice Admiral of the Red, G.C.T.S.   12 Aug. 1819.

*BERKELEY, Sir GEORGE HENRY FREDERICK, Colonel, C.T.S.—K.S.W.—K.W.

*BERRY, Sir EDWARD, Bart. Rear Adm. of the White.

*BERTIE, Sir ALBEMARLE, Bart. Admiral of the White.

>Died 24 Feb. 1824.

*BICKERTON, Sir RICHARD HUSSEY, Bart. Admiral of the Red.

*BINGHAM, Sir GEORGE RIDOUT, Major General, C.T.S.

BLACKWOOD, Sir HENRY, Bart. Vice Admiral of the Red. 12 Aug. 1819.

*BLAIR, Sir ROBERT, Lieutenant General E.I.C.S.

*BLAKENEY, Sir EDWARD, Major General, K.T.S.

*BOUVERIE, Sir HENRY F. Major General.

BOWSER, Sir THOMAS, Lieutenant General E.I.C.S.

*BRADFORD, Sir THOMAS, Lieutenant General, C.T.S.

*BRADFORD, Sir HENRY H. Lieutenant Colonel, K.S.W.—K.W.

>Died 17 Dec. 1817.

*BRENTON, Sir JAHLEEL, Bart. Captain R.N.

*BRISBANE, Sir THOMAS, Lieutenant General.

*BRISBANE, Sir CHARLES, Rear Admiral of the Red.

*BROKE, Sir PHILIP BOWES. (See VERE.)

*BROKE, Sir CHARLES, Lieutenant Colonel.

>Died about 1822.

BROWN, Sir THOMAS, Major General E.I.C.S. 26 July, 1823.

*BROWN, Sir GEORGE SACKVILLE, Major General E.I.C.S.

>Died 1 Jan. 1828.

*BUNBURY, Sir HENRY EDWARD, Bart. Major General.

*BURLTON, Sir GEORGE, Rear Admiral of the White.
        Died 22 Sept. 1815.

*BYNG, Sir JOHN, Lieut. Gen. K.M.T.—K.S.W.

*CALDER, Sir ROBERT, Bart. Admiral of the White.
        Died August or Sept. 1818.

*CAMPBELL, Sir GEORGE, Admiral.
        Died 23 Jan. 1821.

*CAMPBELL, Sir HENRY FREDERICK, Lieutenant General, G.C.H.

*CAMPBELL, Sir COLIN, Major General, K.M.T.—
        K.S.G.—K.M.J.—C.T.S.

CAMPBELL, Sir ALEXANDER, Knt. and Bart.
        Died 11 Dec. 1824.

CAMPBELL, Sir JAMES, Major General, K.T.S.   3
        Dec. 1822.

*CAMPBELL, Sir ARCHIBALD, Portuguese Service,
        C.T.S.
        Nom. Grand Cross 26 Dec. 1826.

*CAMERON, Sir ALAN, Lieutenant General.

*CAMERON, Sir JOHN, Major General, K.T.S.

*CARNCROSS, Sir JOSEPH, Colonel of the Royal Artillery.

*CARR, Sir HENRY WILLIAM, Lieut. Col. K.T.S
Died 18 Aug. 1821.

*CHALMERS, Sir JOHN, Major General E.I.C.S.
Died about 1818.

*COCKBURN, Sir GEORGE, Vice Admiral.
Nom. Grand Cross 20 Feb. 1818.

*CODRINGTON, Sir EDWARD, Rear Admiral, G.C.S.L.
and K.S.G. Nom. Grand Cross 1827.

*COLBORNE, Sir JOHN, Major General..

*COLE, Sir CHRISTOPHER, Knt. Captain R.N. K.M.T.
K.S.G.

*COLLIER, Sir GEORGE RALPH, Bart. Capt. R.N.
Died March, 1824.

*COLVILLE, Lieutenant General Hon. Sir CHARLES,
C.T.S.
Nom. Grand Cross 7 April, 1815.

COOKE, Sir GEORGE, Lieutenant General, K.S.G.
K.W. 16 Sept. 1815.

*DALLAS, Sir THOMAS, Lieutenant General, E.I.C.S.

DARBY, Sir HENRY D'ESTERRE. 20 May, 1820.
Died 1823 or 4.

*DE LANCEY, Sir WILLIAM HOWE, Colonel and De-
puty Quarter Master General. Killed at Waterloo.

DI BORGO, General POZZO, (honorary,) Russian service.

*DICKSON, Sir JEREMIAH, Colonel.

*DICKSON, Sir ALEXANDER I. Col. Royal Artil. K.C.H.

DISNEY, Sir MOORE, Lieutenant General.
        Nom. 7 April, 1815.

DIXON, Sir MANLEY, Admiral of the Blue.
        Nom. 12 Aug. 1819.

*DOMETT, Sir WILLIAM.
        Nom. Grand Cross 16 May, 1820.

DONKIN, Sir RUFANE SHAW, G.C.H.   14 Oct. 1818.

*DORNBERG, Major General Sir W. DE, G.C.H. late
        German Legion, (honorary.)

DOVETON, Sir JOHN, Major General E.I.C.S.
        Nom. 26 Nov. 1819.

*DOUGLAS, Sir WILLIAM, Colonel 91st Foot.
        Died 25 Aug. 1818.

*DOUGLAS, Sir JAMES, Colonel.

*DOWNES, The Right Hon. ULYSSES Lord, Colonel.

*DOYLE, Sir JOHN MILLEY, Colonel, K.T.S.

*D'OYLEY, Sir FRANCIS, Lieutenant Colonel.
        Killed at Waterloo.

*DRUMMOND, Sir GORDON.
        Nom. Grand Cross 7 Jan. 1817.

*DUNDAS, Hon. Sir HENRY ROBERT LAWRENCE, Co-
        lonel, K.C.H. and K.T.S.

*D'URBAN, Sir BENJAMIN, Major General, K.C.H.
        and C.T.S.

*DURHAM, Sir PHILIP CHARLES, Vice Admiral of
        the Red.   Comm. of Military Merit of France.

*DYER, Sir JOHN, Colonel of the Royal Artillery.
> Died 3 July, 1816.

*ELLEY, Sir JOHN, Major Gen. K.M.T. and K.S.G.
*ELLIS, Sir HENRY WALTON, Colonel.
> Killed at Waterloo.
*ESSINGTON, Sir WILLIAM, Vice Admiral.
> Died 12 July, 1816.
*EXMOUTH, The Right Hon. EDWARD Viscount.
> Nom. Grand Cross 16 March, 1816.
*EYRE, Sir GEORGE, Knt. Rear Admiral of the Red.

FAHIE, Sir WILLIAM CHARLES, Rear Admiral of the
> Red, C.F.M.
> > Nom. 13 Jan. 1825.
*FANE, Sir HENRY, Major General,
> Nom. Grand Cross 24 Jan. 1826.
*FERGUSON, Sir RONALD CRAUFURD, Lieutenant Ge-
> neral.
*FLOYER, Sir AUGUSTUS, Colonel E.I.C.S.
> Died 1819.
*FOLEY, Sir THOMAS, Admiral of the Blue.
> Nom. Grand Cross 16 May, 1820.

*FRAMINGHAM, Sir HAYLETT, Col. Royal Artillery.
    Died 10 May, 1820.
*FRASER, Sir AUGUSTUS, Colonel Royal Artillery.
*FREMANTLE, Sir THOMAS FRANCIS, Rear Admiral,
    C.M.T. and G.C.F.M.
        Nom. Grand Cross 20 Feb. 1818.
        Died 19 Dec. 1819,

*GAMBIER, The Right Hon. JAMES Lord, Admiral of
    the Red.
        Nom. Grand Cross 7 June, 1815.
*GARDINER, Sir ROBERT, Lieutenant Colonel, K.S.A.
*GARDNER, ALAN HYDE Lord, Vice Admiral of the
    White.
        Died 27 Dec. 1815.
*GIBBS, Sir SAMUEL, Major General.
        Killed at New Orleans, 1815.
*GILLESPIE, Sir ROBERT ROLLO, Major General.
        Killed at Fort Kalunga, in the East Indies,
        1815.
*GOMM, Sir WILLIAM, Lieutenant Colonel, K.S.A.
*GORDON, Sir JAMES WILLOUGHBY, Lieutenant Ge-
    neral.
*GORDON, Sir JAMES ALEXANDER, Captain R.N.
*GORDON, Hon. Sir ALEXANDER, Lieutenant Colonel.
    Killed at Waterloo.

*GORE, Sir JOHN, Vice Admiral of the Red.

GOULD, Sir DAVIDGE, Admiral of the Blue.
    Nom. 12 June, 1815.

*GRANT, Sir COLQUHOUN, Major General, G.C.H.
    —K.S.W.—K.W.

*GRANT, Sir MAXWELL, Lieutenant Colonel, K.T.S.
    Died Oct. 1823.

GRANT, Sir WILLIAM KEIR, Knt. Lieutenant General and K.M.T.
    Nom. 3 Dec. 1822.

*GREVILLE, Hon. Sir CHARLES J. Major General.

GREY, Sir GEORGE, Bart. Captain R.N.
    Nom. 20 May, 1820.

*GRINDALL, Sir RICHARD, Vice Admiral of the Red.
    Died 1819.

*HALKETT, Sir COLIN, Major General, K.M.J. and K.W.

*HALLOWELL, Sir BENJAMIN, Vice Admiral of the Red and C.F.M.

*HALSTED, Sir LAWRENCE WILLIAM, Vice Admiral of the Red.

*HAMILTON, Sir EDWARD, Bart. Rear Admiral of the White.

*HARDINGE, Sir HENRY, Colonel.

*HARDY, Sir THOMAS MASTERMAN, Bart. Rear Admiral of the Blue.

*HARGOOD, Sir WILLIAM, Vice Admiral of the Red.

*HARTMANN, Lieutenant Colonel Sir JULIUS, K.C.H. late German Legion, (honorary.)

*HERTZBERG, Lieutenant Colonel F. A. (honorary.)

*HERVEY, Sir ELIAB.
      Nom. Grand Cross 1825.

*HILL, Sir THOMAS NOEL, Col. K.T.S. and K.M.J.

*HINUBER, Lieutenant General Sir H. K.C.H. (honorary.)

HISLOP, Sir THOMAS, Major General. 5 Sept. 1818.
      Nom. Grand Cross 14 Oct. 1818.

*HOLMES, Sir GEORGE, Major General E.I.C.S.
      Died 20 Oct. 1816.

*HOPE, Sir GEORGE JOHNSTONE, Rear Admiral.
      Died 2 May, 1818.

*HOPE, Sir JAMES ARCHIBALD, Lieutenant Colonel.

*HOPE, Sir WILLIAM JOHNSTONE, K.S.
      Nom. G.C. 4 Oct. 1825.

*HORSFORD, Sir JOHN, Major General E.I.C.S.
      Died 20 April, 1818.

*HOSTE, Sir WILLIAM, Bart. K.M.T.

*HOTHAM, Hon. Sir HENRY, Vice Admiral of the Red.

*HOTHAM, Sir WILLIAM, Vice Admiral of the Red.

*HOUSTOUN, Sir WILLIAM, Lieutenant General.

*HOWARD OF EFFINGHAM, Lord, C.T.S.
      Nom. Grand Cross 17 March, 1820.

*HOWORTH, Sir EDWARD, K.C. and G C.H.
  Died 5 March, 1827.

*JACKSON, Sir RICHARD DOWNES, Major General.
INGLIS, Sir WILLIAM, Lieutenant General. 7 April,
  1815.
JONES, Sir R. Lieutenant General E.I.C.S. 3 Feb.
  1817.

*KEANE, Sir JOHN, Major General.
*KEMPT, Sir JAMES, Major General, G.C.H.—K.M.T.
  K.S.G. and K.W.
      Nom. G.C. 9 Sept. 1815.
*KING, Sir RICHARD, Vice Admiral of the White.
*KNIGHT, Sir JOHN, Admiral of the White.

*LAFOREY, Sir FRANCIS, Bart. Vice Adm. of the Red.
*LAMBERT, Sir JOHN, Lieutenant General.
LAMOTTE, Lieutenant General, Bavarian Service, (ho-
  norary.) 1819.

*LAVIE, Sir THOMAS, Captain R.N.
   Died 1823.

*LEE, Sir RICHARD, Vice Admiral of the White.

*LEGGE, Hon. Sir ARTHUR KAYE, Vice Admiral of
   the Red.

*LEITH, Sir ALEXANDER, Colonel, C.T.S. and Grand
   Cordon of the Order of Military Merit of France.

*LIND, Sir JAMES, Captain R.N.
   Died about 1823.

*LINSINGEN, Lieutenant General Count, G.C.H. (ho-
   norary.)

*LOW, Major General Baron, (honorary.)

LOWE, Sir HUDSON, Knt. Major General, K.S.G. and
   K.M.P. 23 Jan. 1816.

*LUMLEY, Hon. Sir WILLIAM, Lieutenant General.

LYON, Sir JAMES, Major General, C.S. C.M.J. K.W.
   7 April, 1815.

*MACARA, Sir ROBERT, Lieutenant Colonel.
   Killed at Waterloo.

*MACDONALD, Sir JOHN, Lieutenant General E.I.C.S.
   Died about 1824.

MACFARLANE, Sir ROBERT, Lieut. General, G.C.F.M.
   11 March, 1827.

*MACLEAN, Sir JOHN, Major General, K.T.S.

*MACLEAN, Sir HECTOR, Lieutenant General E.I.C.S.

Mc MAHON, Sir THOMAS, Bart. Major General, 1827.

MAITLAND, Sir PEREGRINE, Major General. 16 Sept. 1815.

*MALCOLM, Sir PULTENEY, Vice Admiral of the Red.

*MALCOLM, Sir JAMES, Lieut. Colonel Royal Marines.

MALCOLM, Sir JOHN, Colonel E.I.C.S. K.L.S.
Nom. Grand Cross 26 Nov. 1819.

MARSHALL, Sir DYSON, Major General E.I.C.S. 14 Oct. 1818.
Died about 1827.

*MARTIN, Sir GEORGE, Admiral of the Blue, G.C. St. Januarius.
Nom. Grand Cross 23 Feb. 1821.

*MARTIN, Sir THOMAS BYAM, Vice Admiral of the Red, K.S.

*MARTINDELL, Sir GABRIEL, Lieutenant General E.I.C.S.

*MAY, Sir JOHN, Lieutenant Colonel Royal Artillery, K.C.H.—K.T.S.—K.S.A.

MILNE, Sir DAVID, Vice Admiral of the Red, Kt. St. Januarius.—C.W. 19 Sept. 1816.

*MITCHELL, Sir WILLIAM, Vice Admiral of the White.
Died 7 March, 1816.

MONTRESOR, Sir HENRY TUCKER, Lieutenant General, G.C.H. 21 March, 1820.

*MOORE, Sir GRAHAM, Vice Admiral of the White.

*MOORSOM, Sir ROBERT, Vice Admiral of the Red.

*MORRIS, Sir JAMES NICOLL, Vice Admiral of the Red.

*MUFFLING, Major General Baron de, Prussian ser-
        vice, (honorary.)

MUNRO, Sir THOMAS, Major General E.I.C.S.   26
        Nov. 1819.   Created a Baronet 1825.
            Died at Madras, 1827.

*MURRAY, Sir GEORGE, Vice Admiral of the Red.
            Died about 1819.

*NAGLE, Sir EDMUND, Admiral of the Blue, G.C.H.

*NEALE, Sir HARRY.
            Nom. Grand Cross 14 Sept. 1822.

NICOLLS, Sir JASPER, Major General.   26 Dec. 1826.

NICHOLLS, Sir HENRY, Admiral of the Blue.   20
        May, 1820.

*NIGHTINGALL, Sir MILES, Lieutenant General.

*NUGENT, Lieutenant General Count, Austrian ser-
        vice, (honorary.)

*O'CALLAGHAN, Hon. Sir ROBERT WILLIAM, Major
        General.

*OCHTERLONY, Sir DAVID, Major General E.I.C.S.
            Nom. Grand Cross 10 Dec. 1816.
            Died 15 July, 1825.

*OSWALD, Sir JOHN, Major General.
> Nom. G.C. 25 Feb. 1824.

OTWAY, Sir ROBERT WALKER, Rear Admiral of the
> Red. 8 June, 1826.

*OWEN, Sir EDWARD-WILLIAM-CAMPBELL-RICH,
Rear Admiral of the Blue.

*PACK, Sir DENNIS, Major General, C.T.S. K.M.T.
and K.S.W.
> Died 24 July, 1823.

*PAULETT, Lord HENRY, Vice Admiral of the White.

*PELLEW, Sir ISRAEL, Vice Admiral of the Red.

PENROSE, Sir CHARLES VINICOMB, Vice Admiral of
the White, G.C.M.G. and G.C.F.M. 3 Jan.
1816.

*POLE, Sir CHARLES MAURICE, Bart. Admiral of the
Red.
> Nom. Grand Cross 20 Feb. 1816.

*POPHAM, Sir HOME RIGGS, Rear Admiral of the
Red, K.M.
> Died 11 Sept. 1820.

*POWER, Sir MANLEY, Major General, C.T.S.
> Died 1825.

*PONSONBY, Hon. Sir WILLIAM, Major General.
> Killed at Waterloo.

*PRATT, Sir CHARLES, Major General.

*PRINGLE, Sir WILLIAM H. Lieutenant General.

PRITZLER, Sir THEOPHILUS, Major General.   3 Dec.
        1822.

REEDE, General DE, Dutch service, (honorary.) 1819.

REYNELL, Sir THOMAS, Major General.   26 Dec. 1826.

*ROBE, Sir WILLIAM, Colonel Royal Artillery, K.C.H.
        and C.T.S.
            Died 1 Nov. 1820.

*ROBINSON, Sir FREDERICK PHILLIPS, Lieutenant
        General.

*ROSS, Sir HEW DALRYMPLE, Lieutenant Colonel
        Royal Artillery, K.T.S.—K.S.A.

*ROWLEY, Sir JOSIAS, Bart. Vice Admiral of the Red.

*ROWLEY, Sir CHARLES, Vice Admiral of the Red,
        K.M.T.

*SAWYER, Sir HERBERT, Admiral of the Blue.

*SCOVELL, Sir GEORGE, Colonel, K.S.W.

*SEYMOUR, Sir MICHAEL, Bart. Captain R.N.

*SMITH, Sir WILLIAM SYDNEY, Admiral of the Blue,
        G.C.S.—K.C.—G.C.F.M.—G.C.T.S. and K.M.

SMITH, Sir LIONEL, Major General.   3 Dec. 1822.

*SOMERSET, Lord ROBERT EDWARD, Lieutenant General, K.T.S.—K.M.T.—K.S.W.

*SOMERSET, Lord FITZROY, Major General, C.T.S.—K.S.G.—K.M.T.—K.M.J.

*STAINES, Sir THOMAS, Knt. Captain R.N.

*STOPFORD, Hon. Sir ROBERT, Admiral of the Blue.

*STOPFORD, Hon. Sir EDWARD, Lieutenant General, K.T.S.

*STOVIN, Sir FREDERICK, Lieutenant Colonel.

*SUTTON, Sir JOHN, Admiral of the Blue.
        Died 8 Aug. 1825.

*SUTTON, Sir CHARLES, Knt. Colonel and C.T.S.
        Died 26 March, 1828.

*TALBOT, Sir JOHN, Rear Admiral of the Red.

TARLETON, Sir BANASTRE, Bart.
        Nom. Grand Cross 1820.

*THOMPSON, Sir THOMAS BOULDEN, Bart. R.N.
        Nom. Grand Cross 14 Sept. 1822.
        Died 3 March, 1828.

*THORNBROUGH, Sir EDWARD, Admiral.
        Nom. Grand Cross 11 Jan. 1825.

TOONE, Sir WILLIAM, Major General E.I.C.S.   26 Nov. 1819.
        Died about 1823.

o

*TORRENS, Sir HENRY, Major General, C.T.S.

*TRENCH, Hon. Sir ROBERT LE POER, Colonel and
K.T.S.
Died March, 1224.

TROLLOPE, Sir HENRY, Admiral of the Red. 20
May, 1820.

*TUCKER, Sir EDWARD, Captain R.N.

*TYLER, Sir CHARLES, Admiral of the Blue.

*VANDELEUR, Sir JOHN ORMSBY, Lieutenant Gene-
ral, K.M.J.—K.S.W.

*VERE, Sir PHILIP BOWES BROOKE, Bart. Captain
R.N.

*VERE, Sir CHARLES BROOKE, Lieutenant Colonel.
K.T.S.—K.S.W.—K.W.

VINCENT, General Baron, Austrian service, (honorary.) 1819.

*VIVIAN, Sir RICHARD HUSSEY, Bart. Major Gene-
ral, K.M.T.—K.S.W.

*WALE, Sir CHARLES, Lieutenant General.

*WALKER, Sir GEORGE TOWNSHEND, Lieutenant General, C.T.S.

 Nom. Grand Cross 1817.

*WALMODEN, Lieutenant General Count, Prussian sevrice, (honorary.)

*WARDE, Sir HENRY, Lieutenant General.

WELLS, Sir JOHN, Admiral of the Blue. 20 May, 1820.

*WHITE, Sir HENRY, Major General E.I.C.S.

 Died 1823.

*WHITSHEAD, Sir JAMES HAWKINS, Admiral of the Red.

WHITTINGHAM, Sir SAMUEL FORD, Major General, K.C.H. 26 Dec. 1826.

*WILLIAMS, Sir THOMAS, Knt. Vice Admiral of the Red.

*WILLIAMS, Sir WILLIAM, Colonel, K.T.S.

*WILLIAMS, Sir RICHARD, Lieutenant Colonel Royal Marines.

*WILLIAMS, Sir EDMUND KEYNTON, Lieutenant Colonel, K.T.S.

*WILSON, Sir JAMES, Lieutenant Colonel.

*WOOD, Sir GEORGE, Major General E.I.C.S.

 Died 1824.

*YEO, Sir JAMES LUCAS, Bart. Knt. of St. Bento
    D'Avis.
        Died 1818.

*YORKE, Sir JOSEPH SYDNEY, Vice Admiral of the
    Red.

KNIGHTS OF
THE MOST ILLUSTRIOUS ORDER
OF ST. PATRICK.

This Order was founded by His late Majesty King GEORGE III.; the number limited to fifteen, exclusive of the Sovereign and the Lord Lieutenant for the time being, who during the continuance of his Government is Grand Master. No extra Knights appear to have been appointed till 1821, when His MAJESTY was pleased to nominate Six, *viz.* H. R. H. the Duke of Cumberland, and the Earls of Ormonde, Meath, Fingal, Courtown, and Roden.

The original Knights of this Order were—

H. R. H. EDWARD Duke of KENT. Died 23 Jan. 1820.

W. ROBERT Duke of LEINSTER. Died 20 Oct. 1805.

HENRY Earl of CLANRICKARDE. Died 8 Dec. 1797.

RANDAL Earl of ANTRIM. (Declined, and the Earl of ARRAN was nominated in his place.)

THOMAS Earl of WESTMEATH. Died 7 Sept. 1791.

MURROUGH Earl of INCHIQUIN. Afterwards Marquess of THOMOND. Died 10 Feb. 1808.

CHARLES Earl (afterwards Marquess) of DROGHEDA.
Died 22 Dec. 1821.

GEORGE Earl of TYRONE, afterwards Marquess of
WATERFORD. Died 3 Dec. 1801.

RICHARD Earl of SHANNON. Died 20 May, 1807.

JAMES Earl of CLANBRASSIL. Died 6 Feb. 1798.

RICHARD Earl of MORNINGTON, now Marquess of
WELLESLEY. Resigned on being elected K.G.
1810.—He is the only survivor of the original
Knights.

JAMES Earl of COURTOWN. Died 30 March, 1810.

JAMES Earl of CHARLEMONT. Died 4 Aug. 1799.

THOMAS Earl of BECTIVE, afterwards Marquess of
HEADFORT. Died 14 Feb. 1795.

HENRY Earl of ELY. Died 8 May, 1793.

ARTHUR Earl of ARRAN. Died 8 Oct. 1809.

Knights nominated since 1783.

Earl of CALEDON. 1821.

JOHN JOSHUA Earl of CARYSFORT. 1784.

WILLIAM HENRY Earl of CLERMONT. 1794. Died
22 March, 1806.

HENRY Marquess of CONYNGHAM. 1801.

JAMES GEORGE Earl of COURTOWN. 1821.

H. R. H. ERNEST AUGUSTUS Duke of CUMBERLAND.
1821.

GEORGE AUGUSTUS Marquess of DONEGAL. 1821.

CHARLES Viscount DILLON. 1798. Died 9 Nov. 1813.

CHARLES Marquess of ELY. 1794. Died 22 March, 1806.

JOHN Marquess of ELY. 1807.

JOHN WILLOUGHBY Earl of ENNISKILLEN. 1814.

ARTHUR JAMES Earl of FINGAL. 1821.

THOMAS Marquess of HEADFORT. 1800.

THOMAS Earl of LONGFORD. 1814.

JOHN Earl of MEATH. 1821.

CHARLES HENRY Earl O'NEIL. 1809.

JAMES W. Marquess of ORMONDE. 1821.

ROBERT Earl of RODEN. 1805. Died 29 June, 1820.

ROBERT Earl of RODEN. 1821.

HENRY Earl of SHANNON. 1809.

JOHN DENIS Marquess of SLIGO. 1805. Died 2 Jan. 1809.

HOWE, PETER, Marquess of SLIGO. About 1814.

CHARLES CHETWYND Earl TALBOT. 1821.

WILLIAM Marquess of THOMOND. About 1814.

IRISH KNIGHTS BACHELORS,

Created by the LORDS LIEUTENANTS or LORDS JUS-
TICES for the time being, and by His Present
MAJESTY, during his visit to that Kingdom, 1821.

For this list the Editor is obliged to his friend, Sir William
Betham, Knt. Ulster King of Arms, and James Rock, Esq.
Dublin Herald.

ALLEY, GEORGE, M.D.   27 April, 1811.

ARMSTRONG, FREDERICK, Captain in the Army.   28
April, 1819.   K.T.S.

BAILLIE, EWEN.   16 July, 1793.

BATEMAN, JOHN, of Waterford.   10 March, 1810.

BETHAM, WILLIAM, Ulster King of Arms.   15 July
1812.

BRADY, NICHOLAS, Sheriff of Dublin.   Sept. 1821.
(By the King in Person.)

BURGOYNE, JOHN.   24 Dec. 1810.

CARR, JOHN, of the Middle Temple, London. 9 Dec. 1808.

CLARKE, ARTHUR. 1811.

DE BEAUVOIR, JOHN, eldest son of Sir John Edmund Browne, Bart. March, 1827.

EUSTACE, JOHN ROWLAND, Captain 19th Dragoons. 4 Feb. 1816. Now Lieutenant Colonel.

FLETCHER, WILLIAM ALEXANDER, of Londonderry. 9 Sept. 1811.

GERARD, MARK ANTHONY, Captain Royal Marines. 30 Aug. 1809.

GRANT, RICHARD, Captain R.N. 1820.

GREY, THOMAS, of Slane Castle, co. Meath, M.D. F.R.S. L.S. 30 Oct. 1819.

GREEN, JONAS, Recorder of Dublin. Sept. 1821. (By the King in Person.)

HARTE, RICHARD, Mayor of Limerick.   June, 1806.

HASSURD, FRANCIS JOHN, Recorder of Waterford.
        10 March, 1810.

HUNTER, RICHARD, M.D.   30 Sept. 1823.

JAMES, JOHN KINGSTON, Lord Mayor of Dublin.   29
        Dec. 1821.   Now Bart.

JONES, RICHARD, of Clonmell.   4 Sept. 1809.

JONES, CHARLES THOMAS, of Montgomery.   1810.
        Lieutenant R.N.

LEE, JOHN THEOPHILUS, of Brompton, Middlesex.
        19 Dec. 1827.

LEES, EDWARD SMITH, Secretary General of the Post
        Office.   (By the King in Person.)   Sept. 1821.

LEWIN, GREGORY ALLMITT, R.N.   1820.

LILLIE, JOHN SCOTT, Major in the Army.   21 Jan.
        1817.

MACARTNEY, JOHN, of Dublin.   29 April, 1796.

MAC DONNELL, FRANCIS, of Donforth Castle, co
        Kildare.   7 Dec. 1827.

MAGENNIS, JOHN, of Londonderry.   Sept. 1821.
        (By the King in Person.)

MALCOLM, CHARLES, Captain R.N. Commander of
the Yacht. 1823.

MARRETT, CHRISTOPHER, of Limerick. Sept. 1821.
(By the King in Person.)

MASSEY, HUGH, of Limerick. 9 Dec. 1809.

MAY, STEPHEN EDWARD, of Belfast. 20 April, 1816.

MEREDYTH, JOSHUA COLLES. 16 May, 1794.

MORGAN, THOMAS CHARLES, M.D. 17 Sept. 1811.

MORIARTY, THOMAS, M.D. 22 Feb. 1811.

NUGENT, EDMOND, Lord Mayor of Dublin. 1 March,
1828.

O'KELLY, ST. GEORGE, High Sheriff of the County of
Dublin. 23 Jan. 1794.

OULD, FIELDING, M.D. 17 May, 1760.

PARSONS, WILLIAM, Mus. D. Master of the King's
Band, &c. 27 Aug. 1795. Died 1817.

PERRIER, DAVID, of Cork. 27 Aug. 1795.

PERRIER, ANTHONY, High Sheriff of the City of
Cork. 1810.

PHILLIMORE, JOHN, Captain R.N. C.B. 12 Dec.
1821.

PICK, VESIAN, late Mayor of Cork. Sept. 1806.
PURCELL, JOHN, of Cork. 18 June, 1811.

READ, Rev. JOHN. 18 June, 1811.
RICH, GEORGE, Chamberlain of the Household. 30
    Sept. 1823.
RIDDALL, JAMES, Sheriff of Dublin. 25 Oct. 1810.
ROOSE, DAVID CHARLES, High Sheriff of Dublin.
    22 March, 1828.

SCOTTOWE, N. B. 1809.
SMART, GEORGE THOMAS, Organist to His Majesty.
    22 Feb. 1811.
SMITH, Captain WILLIAM AUGUSTUS. 18 June,
    1811.
SMITH, WILLIAM, Sheriff of Dublin. 12 Dec. 1821.
STANLEY, EDWARD, Sheriff of Dublin. 25 Oct. 1810.
STEVENSON, JOHN, Mus. D. 1806.
STOPFORD, JAMES. 7 March, 1815.
SYDNEY, WILLIAM ROBERT, of Woolwich, co. Kent.
    7 Dec. 1827.

TAYLOR, JAMES, Lord Mayor of Dublin. 30 May,
    1765.

VASCHELL, WILLIAM.   1809.

WATSON, FREDERICK, Major in the Army.   26 Feb.
     1819.

WHELAN, THOMAS, Sheriff of Dublin.   12 Dec. 1821.
WHITEFORD, GEORGE, Sheriff of Dublin.   Sept. 1821.
     (By the King in Person.)
WHITEFORD, JOHN R.   7 March, 1811.
WILCOCKS, RICHARD, late Inspector of Police in
     Munster.   1 Dec. 1827.
WILSON, ALEXANDER, M.D. of Bath.   10 May, 1813.
WORTHINGTON, WILLIAM, Alderman of Dublin.   1
     Oct. 1797.

YEATES, THOMAS CHARLES, of Dublin.   1 Dec. 1827.

THE MOST DISTINGUISHED ORDER OF ST. MICHAEL AND ST. GEORGE.

Instituted 27 April, 1818, for the United States of the Ionian Islands, and for the Island of Malta.

This and the following Order (the Guelphic) having been instituted subsequently to the publication of any English Work on Knighthood, and their details little known, the Author is induced to give a short abstract of their Statutes: that of the Ionian Order is taken from a copy in the possession of Nicholas Harris Nicolas, Esq.

STATUTES OF THE IONIAN ORDER.

PREAMBLE—Recites the Treaties whereby the United States of the Ionian Islands were placed under the sole protection of, and the Island of Malta ceded in entire sovereignty to the Crown of England, declaring the King's pleasure to found an Order of Knighthood for these Islands, and describes the Great Seal of the Order.

STATUTE I. The King of the United Kingdom of Great Britain and Ireland to be perpetual Sovereign of the Order.

II. The Lord High Commissioner of the United States of the Ionian Islands for the time being, to be Grand Master.

III. The Order to consist of Three Classes :—

Knights GRAND CROSSES. Number, Eight, including the Grand Master.

Knights COMMANDERS. Number, Twelve.

KNIGHTS. Number, Twenty-four.

And providing that each and every person admitted into this Order, shall immediately be entitled to assume the distinctive appellation of Knighthood.

IV. All Members of this Order to be natives of the Ionian Islands or Malta, with power reserved to the Crown to appoint such British-born subjects as should hold " the highest and most confidential situations" in the Ionian Islands or Malta, or in the King's service therein, or the King's Naval Service in the Mediterranean.

V. Appoints that the Commander-in-Chief of the British Naval Forces in the Mediterranean for the time being, shall be First and Principal Grand Cross, but only during the time of his command, at the conclusion of which he is to deliver the Insignia to his successor.

No British subject on whom, in consequence of his

employment in the Ionian Islands or Malta, the Order may be conferred, to continue a Member of the Order, or to retain the Insignia thereof, after he shall cease to be in the said employment, unless he shall actually have been so employed for five years. Absence on leave to be considered as service.

VI.   Describes the Habits and Decorations of the Knights.

VII.   Ceremonial of Investiture.

VIII.   St. George's Day, 23 April, to be observed as the Festival of the Order.

IX.   Members of this Order to take precedence of all Knights Bachelors in the Ionian Islands.

X.   Directs that there shall be two Prelates of this Order, *viz.* the Archbishop Metropolitan of the Ionian Islands, and the Archbishop of Malta, a Registrar, King of Arms, and Secretary.

KNIGHTS OF THE IONIAN ORDER.

ENGLISH KNIGHTS.

H. R. H. Augustus Frederick Duke of Cambridge, K.G. &c. Grand Master. Appointed 1826.

GRAND CROSSES.

Sir Thomas Maitland, G.C.B. Commander of the Forces in the Mediterranean, and Grand Master, 1818, till his death, 1824.

Sir Frederick Adam, K.C.B. Lord High Commissioner of the United States of the Ionian Islands, and Grand Master, 1824 to 1826.

The Right Hon. Frederick Earl of Guilford, Chancellor of the University of the Ionian Islands. Died 14 Oct. 1827.

Vice Admiral Sir Vinicomb Penrose, K.C.B. sometime Commander-in-Chief of the Naval Forces in the Mediterranean.

P

Vice Admiral Sir HARRY NEALE, G.C.B. sometime Commander-in-Chief of the Naval Forces in the Mediterranean.

Vice Admiral Sir EDWARD CODRINGTON, G.C.B. Commander-in-Chief of the Naval Forces in the Mediterranean.

COMMANDERS.

Sir FREDERICK HANKEY, Lieutenant Colonel, sometime Secretary to the Lord High Commissioner.

Sir PATRICK ROSS, Major General, sometime Resident for the Lord High Commissioner at Zante.

Sir FREDERICK STOVIN, sometime Resident for the Lord High Commissioner at Santa Maura.

Sir ROBERT TRAVERS, Colonel and C.B. sometime Inspecting Field Officer of Militia in the Ionian Islands.

Sir RICHARD PLASKETT, sometime Secretary to the Primary Council of the Ionian Islands, and Government Secretary at Malta.

Hon. Sir ANTHONY MAITLAND, Captain R.N. sometime Commodore commanding the Naval Forces in the Mediterranean.

Sir ALEXANDER WOOD, sometime Chief Secretary at Malta.

THE ROYAL HANOVERIAN GUELPHIC ORDER.

This Order was founded by His present MAJESTY, when Prince Regent, 12 August, 1815. The following Abstract of the Statutes is taken from a Translation recently edited by Nicholas Harris Nicolas, Esq. and privately printed for the use of the Members of the Order.*

STATUTES OF THE GUELPHIC ORDER.

The PREAMBLE recites, that His late Majesty, King George III. had contemplated the instituting an Order for Hanover, but had been prevented by the occupation of it by the French Armies, and that His Royal Highness seizes the moment of their returning under his sway, to carry into effect what his Father had intended.

* 4to. 1828. Pickering, Chancery Lane.

The STATUTES follow, in Number Twenty-eight.

I.   The Order to be called " THE ORDER OF THE GUELPHS."

II.   The King of Hanover to be Grand Master.

III.   Appoints a Chancellor, Vice Chancellor, and Secretary.

IV. & V.   The Order to consist of GRAND CROSSES, COMMANDERS, and KNIGHTS, unlimited as to numbers, and directs that Medals shall be provided for Non-Commissioned Officers and Privates.

VI.   Persons who have distinguished themselves in a particular manner alone to be admitted into the Order.

VII.   Members of the Order to take precedence of persons of the same rank who are not Members, and if not already Noble, to be invested with the Rank and personal Rights of Nobility.*

VIII.   The Grand Cross to be given only to such as have distinguished themselves in some separate command.

IX.   No Civilian can have the Grand Cross unless he rank with a Major General.

X.   Foreigners may be admitted Extra Members of the Order.

XI. to XV.   Describe the Habits and Insignia, and direct the way of wearing them.

* This to be understood, of course, in the German, not the English signification of the words Noble and Nobility.

XV. A Chapter to be held on the Anniversaries of the Foundation, for investigating the Claims of Military Persons to be admitted into the Order.

XVI. to XXV. Regulate the Forms to be observed in holding such Chapter, and reporting its Proceedings and Recommendations to the Sovereign.

XXVI. The Names and Arms of all the Members of the Order to be affixed in the Church of the Palace of Hanover.

XXVII. The Festival of the Order to be held on the 12th of August, every year, in the City of Hanover.

XXVIII. Directs the strict observance of the foregoing Statutes.

Three supplemental Statutes of the same date, direct that all the Members of the Order shall be of good Descent and Birth, and entitled to coat armour; prescribe the Form in which their Achievements shall be affixed in the Church and Ancient Hall in the Palace at Hanover; and authorise the Knights to surround their Arms with the Motto and Collar of the Order.

KNIGHTS OF THE GUELPHIC ORDER.

For this list the Editor is indebted to the kindness of the Rev. Dr. Kuper, Minister of the German Chapel, St. James's Palace, Domestic Chaplain to H. R. H. the Duchess of Clarence, and Chaplain to the Hanoverian Embassy.

GRAND CROSSES.

ANGLESEY, General HENRY WILLIAM Marquess of, K.G. G.C.B. &c.

ASGILL, Sir CHARLES, Bart. Died 1822.

BENTINCK, General Lord WILLIAM CAVENDISH, G.C.B.

BERESFORD, General Viscount, G.C.B.

BLOOMFIELD, Major General BENJAMIN Lord, G.C.B.

BURGHERSH, Major General Lord.

BURTON, The Hon. Sir FRANCIS NATHANIEL, Lieutenant Governor of Canada.

BYNG, Lieutenant General Sir JOHN, K.C.B.

CALVERT, General Sir HENRY, Bart. Died 3 Sept. 1826.

CAMPBELL, Lieutenant General Sir JAMES, of Inverneil. Died 1819.

CAMPBELL, Lieutenant General Sir HENRY FREDERICK, K.C.B.

CHOLMONDELEY, GEORGE JAMES Marquess. Died 10 April, 1827.

CLANCARTY, RICHARD Earl of, G.C.B.

CLANWILLIAM, RICHARD Earl of.

CLINTON, Lieutenant General Sir HENRY, G.C.B.

COLVILLE, Lieutenant General Hon. Sir CHARLES, G.C.B.

COMBERMERE, General STAPLETON Viscount, G.C.B.

CONYNGHAM, HENRY Marquess of, K.P.

DON, General Sir GEORGE, G.C.B.

DONKIN, Lieutenant General Sir RUFANE SHAW, K.C.B.

FIFE, The Right Hon. JAMES Earl of.

FREMANTLE, Right Hon. Sir WILLIAM HENRY, Treasurer of the Household.

FREMANTLE, Sir THOMAS FRANCIS, G.C.B. Died 19 Dec. 1819.

FULLER, Lieutenant General Sir JOSEPH.

GORDON, Lieutenant General Sir WILLOUGHBY, Bart. K.C.B.

HALKETT, Major General Sir COLIN, K.C.B.

HAMMOND, Lieutenant General Sir THOMAS T.

HAMPDEN, THOMAS Viscount. Died 20 Aug. 1824.

HARRINGTON, General CHARLES Earl of.

HASTINGS, FRANCIS Marquess of, K.G. G.C.B. &c. Died 28 Nov. 1826.

HASTINGS, General Sir CHARLES, Bart. Died 30 Sept. 1823.

HERTFORD, FRANCIS CHARLES Marquess of, K.G.

HILL, Lieutenant General ROWLAND Lord, G.C.B.

HINUBER, Sir HENRY, K.C.B.

HOPE, Lieutenant General Sir JOHN.

HOUSTOUN, Lieutenant General Sir WILLIAM, K.C.B.

HOWARTH, General Sir EDWARD, K.C.B. Died 5 March, 1827.

HULSE, General Right Hon. Sir SAMUEL.

KEMPT, Lieutenant General Sir JAMES, G.C.B.

KNIGHTON, Sir WILLIAM, Bart.

LONDONDERRY, ROBERT Marquess, K.G. Died
    Aug. 1822.
LONDONDERRY, Lieutenant General CHARLES WIL-
    LIAM Marquess, G.C.B.
LYON, Major General Sir JAMES, K.C.B.

MACFARLANE, Lieutenant General Sir ROBERT, K.C.B.
MACKENZIE, General Sir ALEXANDER, Bart.
MACLEOD, Lieutenant General Sir JOHN.
MAITLAND, Sir THOMAS, G.C.B.   Died 17 Jan. 1824.
MAYO, The Right Hon. JOHN Earl of.
MONTRESOR, Lieutenant General Sir HENRY TUCKER,
    K.C.B.
MOUNTCHARLES, The Right Hon. FRANCIS NATHA-
    NIEL Earl of.
MURRAY, Lieutenant General Sir GEORGE, G.C.B.
MURRAY, Lieutenant General Sir JOHN, Bart.   Died
    1827.

NAGLE, Sir EDMUND, Admiral of the Blue, K.C.B.

Rose, The Right Hon. Sir George.

St. Helens, Alleyne Lord, G.C.B.
Strangford, P. C. S. Viscount, G.C.B.

Taylor, Lieutenant General Sir Herbert.
Taylor, Sir Brooke, Envoy Extraordinary to the
        Court of Munich.
Turner, Lieutenant General Sir Hilgrove.

Warren, Sir J. Borlase, Bart. G.C.B.   Died 1822.
Wellington, Arthur Duke of.

KNIGHTS COMMANDERS.

Airey, Lieutenant General Sir George.

Baring, Lieutenant Colonel George, C.B.
Barnard, Major General Sir Andrew F. K.C.B.
Best, Lieutenant Colonel Charles.
Bolton, Lieutenant General Sir Robert.
Brown, Lieutenant Colonel Thomas Henry.

CHURCH, Lieutenant Colonel Sir RICHARD.
COCKBURN, General GEORGE.
CONGREVE, Sir WILLIAM, Bart.
CONROY, Sir JOHN.
COOKE, Colonel Sir HENRY FREDERICK.

DICKSON, Colonel Sir ALEXANDER, K.C.B.
DOYLE, Major General Sir CHARLES W. C.B.
D'URBAN, Major General Sir BENJAMIN, K.C.B.

ELLEY, Major General Sir JOHN, K.C.B.

FRAMINGHAM, Sir HAYLETT, K.C.B. Died 10 May,
1820.

GARDINER, Lieutenant Colonel, K.C.B.
GLENLYON, The Right Hon. JAMES Lord.
GRANT, Major General Sir COLQUHON, K.C.B.
GRANT, Lieutenant General Sir WILLIAM KEIR,
K.C.B.

HALFORD, Sir HENRY, Bart.
HALKETT, Lieutenant Colonel HUGH.
HARVEY, Colonel Sir JOHN, C.B.
HERRIES, Sir WILLIAM LEWIS.

KERRISON, Sir EDWARD, Major General, Bart. C.B.

MACRA, Lieutenant Colonel Sir JOHN.
MARTIN, Lieutenant Colonel DAVID.
MAY, Lieutenant Colonel Sir JOHN, K.C.B.

PAGET, Hon. Sir CHARLES, Rear Admiral.
POPHAM, Sir HOME RIGGS, K.C.B.

QUENTIN, Lieutenant Colonel Sir GEORGE AUGUSTUS.

REYNETT, Lieutenant Colonel Sir JAMES H.
ROBE, Sir WILLIAM, K.C.B.   Died 1 Nov. 1820.
ROBERTSON, Lieutenant Colonel WILLIAM DE.
ROCHE, Colonel Sir PHILIP, K.C.B.

VIVIAN, Major General Sir ROBERT HUSSEY, Bart. K.C.B.

WALLER, Sir JONATHAN WATHEN, Bart.
WATSON, Sir FREDERICK BEILBY, Master of the Household.
WHITTINGHAM, Major General Sir SAMUEL FORD, K.C.B.
WOOD, Major General Sir GEORGE ADAM.

KNIGHTS.

A'COURT, CHARLES ASHE, Lieutenant Colonel.
ALY, CHARLES, Lieutenant Colonel, C.B.
ARENTSCHILDT, Sir VICTOR VON, Major, C.B.

BAYLEY, Sir DANIEL, Consul General in Russia.
BOSSETT, CHARLES P. DE, Lieutenant Colonel, C.B.
BRYCE, Sir ALEXANDER, Colonel, C.B.

CAREY, Captain German Legion.
CHAPMAN, S. R. Colonel C.B.

CHRISTIE, Sir ARCHIBALD, Commissary General of
    Hospitals at Chatham.

DAVISON, Sir WILLIAM, Major.
DEVON, THOMAS BARKER, Captain R.N.

ECKERSLEY, NATHANIEL, Lieutenant Colonel.

FARQUHAR, ARTHUR, Captain R.N. and C.B.
FONBLANQUE, THOMAS, Captain in the Army, and
    Consul at Koningsberg.

GRAEHME, Captain Hanoverian service.
GRANT, Sir JAMES ROBERT, M.D. Inspector of Hos-
    pitals.
GREEN, ANDREW PELLATT, Captain R.N.

HALL, JOHN, Hanoverian Consul.
HALLIDAY, Sir ANDREW, M.D.

HAMILTON, Sir WILLIAM OSBORNE, Lieutenant Colonel. Died 5 June, 1818.
HANNAGAN, R.D.
HARDINGE, RICHARD, Captain Royal Artillery.
HAVELOCK, WILLIAM, Captain in the Army.
HERVEY, WILLIAM, Lieutenant Colonel. Dead.

MAC GLASHNAN, JAMES, Captain K.G.L. Dead.
McDONALD, ARCHIBALD, Lieutenant Colonel, C.B.
McGREGOR, Sir E. I. M. Bart. C.B.
MEADE, ROCHE, Captain in the Army.
MEADE, Sir JOHN, M.D.
MULLER, GEORGE, Lieutenant Colonel, C.B.

NAYLER, Sir GEORGE, Garter King of Arms.

ORD, ROBERT H. Major Royal Artillery.
OSTEN, WILLIAM, Captain in the Army.

REEVES, GEORGE JAMES, Lieutenant Colonel, C.B.
REH, FREDERICK, Lieutenant Colonel, C.B.

SOUTHWELL, Hon. CHARLES, Captain in the Army.

STEPHENSON, BENJAMIN CHARLES, Surveyor General of the Board of Works.

SYMPHER, AUGUSTUS, Lieutenant Colonel and C.B.

THORNHILL, WILLIAM, Lieutenant Colonel and C.B.

THORNTON, C. WADE, Lieutenant Colonel Royal Artillery.

TODD, WILLIAM DARCY, Captain German Legion.

WHINYATES, E. C. Major Royal Artillery.

THE END.

LONDON:
PRINTED BY S. AND R. BENTLEY,
Dorset Street, Fleet Street.

CPSIA information can be obtained at www.ICGtesting.com
Printed in the USA
LVOW052220251011

252037LV00013B/68/P

CW00921325

Wild Ways

WILD WAYS

Zen Poems of Ikkyū

Translated and edited by
John Stevens

SHAMBHALA
Boston & London
1995

Shambhala Publications, Inc.
Horticultural Hall
300 Massachusetts Avenue
Boston, Massachusetts 02115

9   8   7   6   5   4   3   2   1

First Edition
Printed in the United States of America on acid-free paper ∞
Distributed in the United States by Random House, Inc.,
and in Canada by Random House of Canada Ltd

Library of Congress Cataloging-in-Publication Data
Ikkyū, 1394–1481.
    Wild ways: Zen poems of Ikkyu/translated by John Stevens.
        p.   cm.—(Shambhala centaur editions)
    ISBN 1-57062-074-1 (pbk.)
    1. Ikkyū, 1394–1481—Translations into English.   2. Zen poetry,
Chinese—Translations into English.   I. Stevens, John, 1947–   .
II. Title.   III. Series.
PL2698.I35A27   1995   94-44057
895.1′146—dc20   CIP

Contents

Translator's Introduction

Ikkyū, born as the sun rose on the first day of 1394, was rumored to have been sired by the emperor Gokomatsu. His mother, a member of the influential Fujiwara clan, had been one of Gokomatsu's attendants at court, but she had been slandered by the empress and subsequently ousted from the palace prior to Ikkyū's birth.

Being in such straitened circumstances, Ikkyū's mother was obliged to send him at age five to Ankoku-ji, a Rinzai Zen temple in Kyoto, to be raised by the monks. The precocious little acolyte quickly distinguished himself at the monastery, attaining renown at that early age for both his keen mind and his impish behavior. Ikkyū may have been mischievous, but even as a teenager he was deadly serious about Zen. When Ikkyū was fifteen, he overheard the subabbot boasting about his family background and important connections. "Filled with shame," Ikkyū abandoned Ankoku-ji and went to train under Ken'ō, an eccentric old-time master who lived in a shack in the hills.

Ikkyū remained with Ken'ō until the master's death, in 1414. Despondent, the troubled Ikkyū contemplated suicide for a time and then sought admission to the community of monks training with Kasō, another no-nonsense Zen master of the old school. The regimen at Kasō's retreat consisted of heavy work, meager food, little sleep, and endless hours of meditation.

Ikkyū's struggle for awakening was long and arduous, but one midsummer night in 1420, as he was meditating in a boat on lovely Lake Biwa, the caw of a crow brought the twenty-six-year-old monk out of his stupor. Ikkyū's enlightenment verse:

> For twenty years I was in turmoil
> Seething and angry, but now my time has
>   come!
> The crow laughs, an arhat emerges from
>   the filth,
> And in the sunlight a jade beauty sings!

When Kasō presented Ikkyū with an *inka,* a seal of enlightenment, Ikkyū hurled it to the ground in protest and stomped away. Despite this and other difficulties between master and disciple, Kasō said, "Ikkyū is my true heir, but his ways are wild."

After Kasō died, in 1428, Ikkyū indeed went his own wild way, calling himself a "crazy cloud." He spent much of his life as a vagrant monk, wandering here and there in the environs of Kyoto, Nara, Osaka, and Sakai. Ikkyū mingled with all manner of people, from the highest (he had several meetings with the retired emperor Gokomatsu) to the lowest (he often traveled in the company of beggars). Ikkyū was the darling of merchants, who loved his antic style, yet at the same time he was a defender of the poor against greedy landlords. On occasion Ikkyū played Robin Hood— taking money set aside for a rich man's funeral and spending it on the homeless, for example.

Once Ikkyū, clad in his customary shabby robe and tattered hat, went to beg at the door of a wealthy family's home. He was roughly ordered around to the back of the estate and given scraps. The following day, Ikkyū appeared at a vegetarian feast sponsored by the family, but this time Ikkyū was decked out in the brocade robes of an abbot. When the large tray of food was placed before him, Ikkyū removed his stiff robe and arranged it in front of the tray. "What are you doing?" the startled host asked. "The food belongs to the robe, not to me," Ikkyū replied as he got up to leave.

Ikkyū interspersed his travels with lengthy retreats deep in the mountains, where he grew vegetables and meditated. He counted many artists among his wide circle of acquaintances, and Ikkyū's own dynamic art had a profound impact on the development of poetry, painting, calligraphy, the tea ceremony, flower arranging, and Noh drama in Japan. Periodically, Ikkyū was summoned to serve as chief priest of a temple, only to quickly grow disgusted with the hypocrisy of fame-and-fortune Zen:

> Who among Rinzai's descendants really
>   transmits his Zen?
> It is concealed in this Blind Donkey.
> Straw sandals, a bamboo staff, an
>   unfettered life—
> You can have your fancy chairs,
>   meditation platforms, and fame-and-
>   fortune Zen.

Throughout his life, Ikkyū wanted his Zen to be raw, direct, and authentic. For Ikkyū, part of being authentic was to be totally up front about sex: "If one is thirsty, he dreams of water; if one is cold, he will dream of a thick robe. It is my nature to dream of the pleasures of the bedchamber!" After initial experiences with homosexual love in the monastery, Ikkyū turned to women as a constant source of inspiration and unbridled joy. There were also difficult periods of deprivation and intense sorrow in Ikkyū's love life, which he accepted as being equally valid Zen experiences.

Following eight decades of wild ways, in 1474 Ikkyū was asked to become head abbot of Daitoku-ji, perhaps the most important Zen temple in the cultural history of Japan. Daitoku-ji had been destroyed in the senseless Ōnin War, and in seven years Ikkyū succeeded in having it completely rebuilt. The effort exhausted him, however, and Ikkyū passed away while seated in the lotus posture in 1481, at age eighty-seven. Not long before his death he told his disciples:

> After I'm gone, some of you will seclude yourselves in the forests and mountains to meditate, while others may drink rice wine and enjoy the company of women. Both kinds of Zen are fine, but if some become professional clerics, babbling about "Zen as the Way," they are my enemies.*

---

*There are several full-length studies of Ikkyū available in English: Sonya Arntzen, *Ikkyū and the Crazy Cloud Anthology* (Tokyo: University of Tokyo Press, 1988), Jon Covel and Sobin Yamada, *Zen's Core: Ikkyū's Freedom* (Seoul: Hollym International, 1980), and J. H. Sanford, *Zen-Man Ikkyū* (Chico, Calif.: Scholar's Press, 1981). See also John Stevens, *Three Zen Masters: Ikkyū, Hakuin, Ryōkan* (Tokyo: Kodansha International, 1993).

Ikkyū began composing poetry in his early teens, and more than a thousand poems are contained in the *Crazy Cloud Anthology (Kyōun-shū)* compiled by his disciples. Just as in everything else, Ikkyū totally ignored the rules of composition, and his poems come in all styles and forms. Much of his verse rants against the pervasive hypocrisy of the Buddhist establishment and decries the corruption of the imperial court and its officials. Such criticism was entirely justified, but even Ikkyū himself felt that he often went too far—"How many have I slain with my barbed words?" He ranted against himself as well, bemoaning his lack of self-control and his inordinate love of poetry. In addition to poems on standard religious subjects, Ikkyū composed a number of poems on koan phrases (usually his poems are more

difficult to understand than the koans themselves). Ikkyū wrote several prose poems on
Buddhist themes, the best being "Skeletons,"
which is included at the end of this collection.

As a poet, Ikkyū was at his finest when writing about what he loved most: the unfettered
Zen life and the joys of sexual intimacy. The
selection presented here in *Wild Ways* consists
of verses centering around those two themes.
It may seem ironic that a Buddhist monk is
best remembered for his love songs, but we
also have the example of the sixth Dalai Lama,
who once chanted:

> If the bar-girl does not falter,
> The beer will flow on and on.
> This maiden is my refuge
> And this place my haven.

Zen Poems

One Short Pause

One short pause between
The leaky road here and
The never-leaking Way there:
If it rains, let it rain!
If it storms, let it storm!

A Crazy Cloud, out in the open,
Blown about madly, as wild as they come!
Who knows where this cloud will go, where
   the wind will still?
The sun rises from the eastern sea, and shines
   over the land.

Forests and fields, rocks and weeds—my true
   companions.
The wild ways of the Crazy Cloud will never
   change.
People think I'm mad but I don't care:
If I'm a demon here on earth, there is no need
   to fear the hereafter.

Every day, priests minutely examine the
    Dharma
And endlessly chant complicated sutras.
Before doing that, though, they should learn
How to read the love letters sent by the wind
    and rain, the snow and moon.

Monks these days study hard in order to turn
A fine phrase and win fame as talented poets.
At Crazy Cloud's hut there is no such talent,
    but he serves up the taste of truth
As he boils rice in a wobbly old cauldron.

Bliss and sorrow, love and hate, light and
 shadow, hot and cold, joy and anger, self
 and other.
The enjoyment of poetic beauty may well lead
 to hell.
But look what we find strewn all along our
 Path:
Plum blossoms and peach flowers!

Ten days in this temple and my mind is
   reeling!
Between my legs the red thread stretches and
   stretches.
If you come some other day and ask for me,
Better look in a fish stall, a sake shop, or a
   brothel.

Returning to the City from the Mountains

Crazy Cloud blown by who knows what wild
    wind.
In the mountains by day, in the city by night.
I shout KATSU and wield the staff when I see
    fit,
Even Rinzai and Tokusan would be no match
    for me.

    Rinzai (Lin-chi, d. 866) employed thundering Zen
shouts to awaken his students; the motto of Tokusan
(Te-shan, 782–865) was, "Whether you speak or not,
thirty blows of my stick!"

I Hate Incense

A master's handiwork cannot be measured
But still priests wag their tongues explaining
   the "Way" and babbling about "Zen."
This old monk has never cared for false piety
And my nose wrinkles at the dark smell of
   incense before the Buddha.

Crazy Cloud speaks of Daitō's unsurpassed
   brilliance
But the clatter of royal carriages about the
   temple gates drowns him out
And no one listens to tales of the Patriarch's
   long years
Of hunger and homelessness beneath Gojō
   Bridge.

In order to deepen his Zen understanding, Daitō Ko-
kushi (also known as Shūhō Myōchō, 1281–1338), the
founder of Daitoku-ji, passed a number of years hiding
out among the beggars clustered about Kyoto's Gojō
Bridge.

Monk Gantō practiced Zen while rowing a
    boat;
Monk Chin gathered rushleaf to make sandals.
I always praise the great worth of a single
    raincoat and straw hat—
But who is there to appreciate their true
    elegance?

Gantō (Yen-T'ou, 828–88) worked as a ferryman
during the persecution of Buddhism in the ninth century; Chin (Ch'en, 780–877) made and sold straw sandals to support his aged mother.

Raincoat and Straw Hat

Woodcutters and fishermen know just how to
  use things.
What would they do with fancy chairs and
  meditation platforms?
In straw sandals and with a bamboo staff, I
  roam three thousand worlds,
Dwelling by the water, feasting on the wind,
  year after year.

A Fisherman

Studying texts and stiff meditation can make
   you lose your Original Mind.
A solitary tune by a fisherman, though, can be
   an invaluable treasure.
Dusk rain on the river, the moon peeking in
   and out of the clouds;
Elegant beyond words, he chants his songs
   night after night.

Crazy Cloud is a demon in Daitō's line
But he hates the hellish bickering.
What good are old koans and faded traditions?
No use complaining any more, I'll just rely on
    my inner treasures.

Who needs the Buddhism of ossified masters?
Me, I've spent three decades alone in the
   mountains
And solved all my koans there,
Living Zen among the tall pines and high
   winds.

A Moonless Midautumn

No moon on the best night for moon viewing;
I sit alone near the iron candle stand and
    quietly chant old tunes—
The best poets have loved these evenings
But I just listen to the sound of the rain and
    recall the emotions of past years.

My Mountain Monastery

A thatched hut of three rooms surpasses seven
  great halls.
Crazy Cloud is shut up here far removed from
  the vulgar world.
The night deepens, I remain within, all alone,
A single light illuminating the long autumn
  night.

堤茶畑の咡の栢手の花菜

A Hermit Monk in the Mountains

I like it best when no one comes,
Preferring fallen leaves and swirling flowers for
   company.
Just an old Zen monk living like he should,
A withered plum tree suddenly sprouting a
   hundred blossoms.

Lingering Chrysanthemums
in the South Garden

The last chrysanthemums of late autumn fade
    along the east hedge;
I face the southern mountains, my thoughts a
    million miles away.
I know nothing about the Three Essentials or
    Three Mysteries of Zen Buddhism,
Delighting instead in the elegance of Yuan-
    ming's songs.

———————

    The Three Essentials and Three Mysteries are the
philosophical basis of Rinzai Buddhism. T'ao Yuan-
ming was a fifth-century Chinese poet who once wrote
about the wonders of nature, "These things contain the
deepest truth, but we lack the words to express it fully."

Shut up in a hut chanting verse beside a single
    lamp;
A poet-monk just follows nature without a set
    path.
The advent of spring lifts my melancholy a bit,
    but the night is still so chill,
Freezing even the plum blossoms on my
    calligraphy paper!

Relativity

Buddha died just when nature was coming
    back to life:
One sword cleaves cleanly soul and body.
It is hard to obtain Buddhahood that is not
    born and does not die—
Flowers appear and disappear seamlessly in
    spring.

Enlightenment and Delusion

No beginning, no end, this one mind of ours.
The Original Mind cannot become Buddha-
   nature.
Original Buddhahood is Buddha's mischievous
   talk;
The Original Mind of sentient beings is
   nothing but delusion.

My real dwelling
Has no pillars
And no roof either
So rain cannot soak it
And wind cannot blow it down!

Coming alone,
Departing alone,
Both are delusion:
Let me teach you how
Not to come, not to go!

Of all things
There is nothing
More congratulatory
Than a weatherbeaten
Old skull!

I'd like to
Offer something
To help you
But in the Zen School
We don't have a single thing!

Poem Inscribed on a Painting of Bodhidharma

He does not lie down, he does not get up,
He does not think about things.
He does not know,
And if you ask he will say MU!
Even if you do not ask
He will give you MU!
Question or not,
He does not have a word to say.
Honorable Bodhidharma—
What should we keep in our hearts?

My Hovel

The world before my eyes is wan and wasted,
    just like me.
The earth is decrepit, the sky stormy, all the
    grass withered.
No spring breeze even at this late date,
Just winter clouds swallowing up my tiny reed
    hut.

Poem Exchanged for Food

Once again I'm roaming East Mountain
    hungry.
When you are starving, a bowl of rice is worth
    a thousand pieces of gold.
An ancient worthy swapped his wisdom for a
    few lichee nuts,
Yet I still cannot refrain from singing odes to
    the wind and moon.

In Thanks for a Gift
of Soy Sauce

Untrammeled and free for thirty years
Crazy Cloud practices his own brand of Zen.
A hundred flavors spice my simple fare:
Thin gruel and twig tea are part of the True
    Transmission.

Cancel All Debts

Robbers never strike at the homes of the poor;
Private wealth does not benefit the entire
    nation.
Calamity has its source in the accumulated
    riches of a few,
People who lose their souls for ten thousand
    coins.

A Poem of Protest

Over and over,
Taking and taking
From this village:
Starve the farmers
And how will *you* live?

If your meditation cannot work in the Hall of
   Life and Death,
Fame and fortune will captivate you
   completely.
Human beings have a mixed bill of fare to be
   sure:
Sometimes tasty meat stew, sometimes weak
   citrus-rind tea!

Fleeing from Mika-no-hara to Nara to Escape the War

The road I travel is hard, so hard, and I know
    every step.
These mountains and rivers must be like those
    of China.
After traversing ten thousand leagues and
    wading through ten thousand scrolls,
I've learned to savor the poetry of Tu Fu.

Tu Fu (712–770) was Ikkyū's favorite Chinese poet. Even though he held a series of bureaucratic posts, Tu Fu had a hard life, marred by difficult circumstances and long absences from his family and friends. Like Ikkyū, Tu Fu composed candid, intensely personal verse.

Typhoons and floods make everyone suffer,
And tonight there will be no singing and
   dancing.
The Dharma flourishes and decays, ages come
   and go:
So right yet so sad—the bright moon sets
   behind the Western Pavilion.

A Gentleman's Wealth

A poet's treasure consists of words and
    phrases;
A scholar's days and nights are perfumed with
    books.
For me, plum blossoms framed by the window
    is an unsurpassable pleasure;
A stomach tight with cold but still enchanted
    by snow, the moon, and dawn frost.

Fertilizing My Bamboo Grove
with Horse Manure

Look, look, how I nourish the phoenix mind
    of mine:
Swallows, sparrows, pigeons, crows, all birds
    are welcome here.
Rinzai planted pine, Ikkyū cultivates
    bamboo—
Later generations will praise us for really doing
    something.

南蠻渡りの鬼よ
一体どうやつてきたらしい
何しやうとなさない
てんて折りいれのふく
今かううしせたんだらう
どうしてこうごとうへぼ
剛出きるとすなろ
一株より南良とる
此化のなうとる虫
御川間　附川閣
太作部　為六くらの内蔵
あかくとくろう
太よく里らう

A Meal of Fresh Octopus

Lots of arms, just like Kannon the Goddess;
Sacrificed for me, garnished with citron, I
    revere it so!
The taste of the sea, just divine!
Sorry, Buddha, this is another precept I just
    cannot keep.

Honored One of the Forest

I raised a small sparrow that I loved deeply. One day it suddenly died and, grief-stricken by the loss, I decided to conduct a funeral service for my little companion just as if it were a human being. At first I called it Disciple Sparrow, but then upon its death I changed it to Buddha Sparrow. Finally, I presented it with the posthumous Buddhist title, Honored One of the Forest. I composed this poem as a memorial.

A sixteen-foot body of purple and gold
Lies between the twin trees of nirvana.
Now liberated from falsehood, beyond life and
    death,
Yet present in a thousand mountains, ten
    thousand trees, and hundreds of springs.

Nightingale

A bird too chants sutras of salvation
Filling the trees with marvelous tones.
Forest flowers are like Bodhisattvas,
Surrounding a little bird-buddha.

Nature's Way

The wise heathens have no knowledge;
They just keep their mind continually set on
   the Way.
There are no big-shot Buddhas in nature,
And ten thousand sutras are distilled in a
   single song.

The Dreamy Sound
of Bokushitsu's Shakuhachi
Awakened Me from Deep Sleep
One Moonlit Night

A wonderful autumn night, fresh and bright;
Over the echo of music and drums from a
    distant village
The single clear tone of a *shakuhachi* brings a
    flood of tears—
Startling me from a deep, melancholy dream.

Ikkyū was very fond of both playing and listening to
the *shakuhachi*, the Japanese bamboo flute.

Exhausted with gay pleasures, I embrace my
   wife.
The narrow path of asceticism is not for me;
My mind runs in the opposite direction.
It is easy to be glib about Zen—I'll just keep
   my mouth shut
And rely on love play all the day long.

A Man's Root

Eight inches strong, it is my favorite thing;
If I'm alone at night, I embrace it fully—
A beautiful woman hasn't touched it for ages.
Within my *fundoshi* there is an entire universe!

A *fundoshi* is a type of loose-fitting underwear once
worn by Japanese men.

A Woman's Sex

It has the original mouth but remains
    wordless;
It is surrounded by a magnificent mound of
    hair.
Sentient beings can get completely lost in it
But it is also the birthplace of all the Buddhas
    of the ten thousand worlds.

Rinzai's disciples never got the Zen message,
But I, the Blind Donkey, know the truth:
Love play can make you immortal.
The autumn breeze of a single night of love is
  better than a hundred thousand years of
  sterile sitting meditation . . .

Stilted koans and convoluted answers are all
  monks have,
Pandering endlessly to officials and rich
  patrons.
Good friends of the Dharma, so proud, let me
  tell you,
A brothel girl in gold brocade is worth more
  than any of you.

Emerging from the world's grime, a puritan
    saint is still nowhere near a Buddha.
Enter a brothel once and Great Wisdom will
    explode upon you.
Manjushri should have let Ananda enjoy
    himself in the whorehouse—
Now he will never know the joys of elegant
    love play.

Ananda, a favorite disciple of Buddha, was once enchanted by a courtesan and entered a brothel. Manjushri
countered the girl's spell with one of his own, thus sav-
ing Ananda's virtue.

A sex-loving monk, you object!
Hot-blooded and passionate, totally aroused.
Remember, though, that lust can consume all
    passion,
Transmuting base metal into pure gold.

The lotus flower
Is unstained by mud;
This single dewdrop,
Just as it is,
Manifests the real body of truth.

Follow the rule of celibacy blindly and you are
    no more than an ass;
Break it and you are only human.
The spirit of Zen is manifest in ways countless
    as the sands of the Ganges.
Every newborn is a fruit of the conjugal bond.
For how many aeons have secret blossoms
    been budding and fading?

With a young beauty, sporting in deep love
    play;
We sit in the pavilion, a pleasure girl and this
    Zen monk.
Enraptured by hugs and kisses,
I certainly don't feel as if I am burning in hell.

In Praise of Fish-Basket Kannon

Crimson cheeks, light-colored hair, full of
    compassion and love.
Lost in a dream of love play, I contemplate her
    beauty.
Her thousand eyes of great mercy look upon
    all but see no one beyond redemption.
This goddess can even be a fisherman's wife by
    a river or sea, singing of salvation.

Long ago, there was an old woman who had supported a hermit monk for twenty years. She had a sixteen-year-old girl bring him meals. One day she instructed the girl to embrace the monk and ask, "How do you feel right now?" The young girl did as told, and the monk's response was, "I'm an old withered tree against a frigid cliff on the coldest day of winter." When the girl returned and repeated the monk's words to the old woman, she exclaimed. "For twenty years I've been supporting that base worldling!" The old woman chased the monk out and put the hermitage to the torch.

The introduction to this poem relates one of the toughest koans for a Zen practitioner to solve: "Why did the old woman drive the monk out?"

The old woman was bighearted enough
To elevate the pure monk with a girl to wed.
Tonight if a beauty were to embrace me
My withered old willow branch would sprout
   a new shoot!

Poem Presented to My Friend Ako at the Hot Spring

It is nice to get a glimpse of a lady bathing—
You scrubbed your flower face and cleansed
   your lovely body
While this old monk sat in the hot water,
Feeling more blessed than even the emperor of
   China!

When we parted, it broke my heart;
Her powdered cheeks were more beautiful
  than spring flowers.
My lovely miss is now with another,
Singing the same love song but to a different
  tune.

Reminiscences

Memories and deep thoughts of love pain my
    breast;
Poetry and prose all forgotten, not a word left.
There is a path to enlightenment but I've lost
    heart for it.
Today, I'm still drowning in samsara.

The Dharma Master of Love

My life has been devoted to love play;
I've no regrets about being tangled in red
   thread from head to foot,
Nor am I ashamed to have spent my days as a
   Crazy Cloud—
But I sure don't like this long, long bitter
   autumn of no good sex!

For ten straight years, I reveled in pleasure
    houses.
Now I'm all alone deep in the dark mountain
    valley.
Thirty thousand cloud leagues live between me
    and the places I love.
The only sound that reaches my ears is the
    melancholy wind blowing in the pines.

Three Poems on Love
and Longing

Day and night I cannot keep you out of my
  thoughts;
In the darkness, on an empty bed, the longing
  deepens.
I dream of us joining hands, exchanging words
  of love,
But then the dawn bell shatters my reverie and
  rends my heart.

Women, lovely flowers that bloom and quickly
  fade;
Flowery faces, in full flush, lovely as dreams.
When flowers burst open they grow heavy
  with passion

But once they fall, no one speaks of them
    again.

Even if I were a god or a Buddha you'd be on
    my mind.
I sit beneath the lamp, a skinny monk chanting
    love songs.
The fierce autumn wind nearly bowls me over
And my heart is choked with thick clouds.

Under the Fragrant Eaves

The bamboo thicket has a new set of sprouts.
This old monk feels young again,
My beauty is just thirty-six.
A fresh breeze blows through the crumbling
　　walls.

When Ikkyū was in his seventies, he met and fell in
love with the blind minstrel Lady Mori. Their passionate affair is one of the great love stories of Japan.

The Stick of Zen

Sexual love can be so painful when it is deep,
Making you forget even the best prose and
poetry.
Yet now I experience a heretofore unknown
natural joy,
The delightful sound of the wind soothing my
thoughts.

To Lady Mori

The most beautiful and truest of all women;
Her songs the fresh, pure melody of love.
A voice and sweet smile that rends my heart—
I'm in a spring forest of lovely cherry-apples.

Every night, Blind Mori accompanies me in
    song.
Under the covers, two mandarin ducks whisper
    to each other.
We promise to be together forever,
But right now this old fellow enjoys an eternal
    spring.

Lady Mori's Gifted Touch

My hand is no match for that of Mori.
She is the unrivaled master of love play:
When my jade stalk wilts, she can make it
   sprout!
How we enjoy our intimate little circle.

Lady Mori Rides in a Palanquin

My blind love goes riding in a palanquin on
    spring outings.
When I'm sorely distressed she lifts my gloom.
Everyone makes fun of us, but
I love to gaze upon her, an elegant beauty.

Within your bedchamber, emotion for a
    torrent of poems.
Amid the flowers we sing and dance blissfully,
Sporting like mandarin ducks—
Our love play soars to heights unimagined.

Dead winter but our poetry glows;
Drunk after downing cup after cup.
Years since I enjoyed such sweet love play.
The moon disappears, dawn breaks, yet we
    hardly notice.

A Jonquil Flower

The perfume from her narcissus causes my
    bud to sprout, sealing our love pact.
The delicate fragrance of the flower of eros,
A waterborne nymph, she engulfs me in love
    play,
Night after night, by the emerald sea, under
    the azure sky.

みえつる月の
ありやても
うきことは

あくると
ぬるその
ひかりのと
あられへる

僧都源信

My Beauty's Dark Place Is a Fragrant Narcissus

I am infatuated with the beautiful Mori from
    the celestial garden.
Lying on the pillows, tongue on her flower
    stamen,
My mouth fills with the pure perfume of the
    waters of her stream.
Twilight comes, then moonlight shadows, as
    we sing fresh songs of love.

By river or sea, in the mountains,
A man of the Way shuns fame and fortune.
Night after night, we two lovebirds snuggle on
 the meditation platform,
Lost in dalliance, intimate talk, and orgasmic
 bliss.

To Lady Mori with Deepest Gratitude and Thanks

The tree was barren of leaves but you brought
    a new spring.
Long green sprouts, verdant flowers, fresh
    promise.
Mori, if I ever forget my profound gratitude
    to you,
Let me burn in hell forever.

To My Daughter

Even among beauties she is a precious pearl;
A little princess in this sorry world.
She is the inevitable result of true love,
And a Zen master is no match for her!

Ikkyū apparently fathered a love child with Lady
Mori.

Farewell, Lady Mori

Ten years ago beneath the blossoms we began
    a fragrant alliance.
Each stage was a delight, full of endless
    passion.
How poignant, never again to pillow my head
    on her lap.
Making sweet love together, we vowed to be
    together always.

Upon Becoming Abbot
of Daitoku-ji

Daitō's descendants have nearly extinguished
  his light;
After such a long, cold night, the chill will be
  hard to thaw even with my love songs.
For fifty years, a vagabond in a straw raincoat
  and hat—
Now I'm mortified as a purple-robed abbot.

Self-Portrait

The long sword flashes against heaven.
My skeleton exposed for all to see.
Me, I am praised as a general of Zen,
Tasting life and enjoying sex to the fullest!

Death Verse

In this vast realm
Who understands my Zen?
Even if Master Kidō shows up,
He is not worth a cent!

The Chinese master Kidō (Hsü-T'ang, 1185–1269)
was Ikkyū's Zen hero, a no-nonsense, uncompromising
teacher of truth.

Skeletons

These thin lines of India ink reveal all truth.

Students, sit earnestly in *zazen*, and you will realize that everything born in this world is ultimately empty, including oneself and the original face of existence. All things indeed emerge out of emptiness. This original formlessness is "Buddha," and all other similar terms—Buddha-nature, Buddhahood, Buddha-mind, Awakened One, Patriarch, God—are merely different expressions for the same emptiness. Misunderstand this and you will end up in hell.

Filled with disgust and longing to liberate

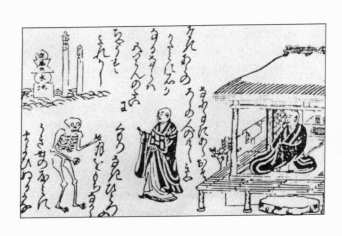

myself from the realm of continual birth and death, I abandoned home and set off on a journey. One night, I came to a lonely little temple, looking for a place to rest. I was far off the main road, at the base of a mountain, seemingly lost in a vast Plain of Repose. The temple was in a field of graves, and suddenly a pitiful-looking skeleton appeared speaking these words:

> A melancholy autumn wind
> Blows through the world:
> The pampas grass waves,
> As we drift to the moor,
> Drift to the sea.

What can be done
With the mind of a man,
That should be clear
But, dressed up in a monk's robe,
He just lets life pass him by?

All things become naught by returning to their origin. Bodhidharma faced the wall in meditation, but none of the thoughts that arose in his mind had any reality. The same holds true for Buddha's fifty years of proclaiming the Dharma. The Mind is not bound by such conditioned things.

Such deep musings made me uneasy and I could not sleep. Toward dawn I dozed off, and in my dreams I found myself surrounded by a bunch of skeletons, acting as they did in life.

One skeleton came over to me and said:

Memories
Flee and
Are no more:
All are empty dreams
Devoid of meaning.

Violate the reality of things
And babble about
"God" and "Buddha"
And you will never find
The true Way.

Still breathing,
You feel animated,
So a corpse in a field
Seems to be something
Apart from you.

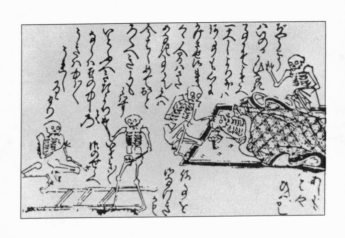

I got on well with this skeleton—he had renounced the world to seek the truth and had passed from the shallows to the depths. He saw things clearly, just the way they are. I lay there with the wind in the pines whispering in my ears and the autumnal moonlight dancing across my face.

What is not a dream? Who will not end up as a skeleton? We appear as skeletons covered with skin, male and female, and lust after each other. When the breath expires, though, the skin ruptures, sex disappears, and there is no more high or low. Underneath the skin of the person we fondle and caress right now is nothing more than a bare set of bones. Think about it—high and low, young and old, male and female, all the same. Awaken to this one great matter and you will immediately comprehend

the meaning of "unborn and undying."

> If chunks of rock
> Can serve as a memento
> To the dead,
> A better headstone
> Would be a tea mortar.

Humans are indeed frightful beings.

> A single moon
> Bright and clear
> In an unclouded sky:
> Yet still we stumble
> In the world's darkness.

Have a good look—stop the breath, peel off the skin, and everybody ends up looking the

same. No matter how long you live, the result is not altered. Cast off the notion that "I exist." Entrust yourself to the windblown clouds, and do not wish to live forever.

> This world
> Is but
> A fleeting dream
> So why be alarmed
> At its evanescence?

Your span of life is set and entreaties to the gods to lengthen it are to no avail. Keep your mind fixed on the one great matter of life and death. Life ends in death, that's the way things are.

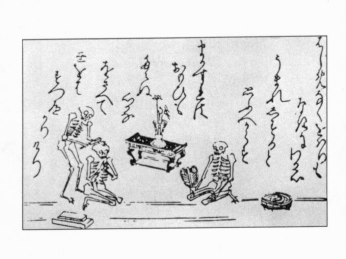

The vagaries of life,
Though painful,
Teach us
Not to cling
To this floating world.

Why do people
Lavish decoration
On this set of bones
Destined to disappear
Without a trace?

The original body
Must return to
Its original place:
Do not search
For what cannot be found.

No one really knows
The nature of birth
Nor the true dwelling place:
We return to the source,
And turn to dust.

Many paths lead from
The foot of the mountain
But at the peak
We all gaze at the
Single bright moon.

If at the end of our journey
There is no final
Resting place
Then we need not fear
Losing our way.

No beginning,
No end;
Our mind
Is born and dies:
The emptiness of emptiness!

Let up
And the mind
Runs wild;
Control the world
And you can cast it aside.

Rain, hail, snow, and ice:
All separate
But when they fall
They become the same water
Of the valley stream.

The ways of proclaiming
The Mind all vary
But the same heavenly truth
Can be seen
In each and every one.

Cover your path
With fallen pine needles
So no one will be able
To locate your
True dwelling place.

How vain
The endless funerals at the
Cremation grounds of Mount Toribe:
Don't the mourners realize
That they will be next?

"Life is fleeting!"
We think at the sight
Of smoke drifting from Mount Toribe:
But when will we realize
That we are in the same boat?

All is vain!
This morning,
A healthy friend;
This evening,
A wisp of cremation smoke.

What a pity!
Evening smoke from Mount Toribe
Blown violently
To and fro
By the wind.

When burned
It becomes ashes,
And earth when buried.
Is it only our sins
That remain behind?

All the sins
Committed
In the Three Worlds
Will fade away
Together with me.

This is how the world is. Those who have
not grasped the world's impermanence are as-
tonished and terrified by such change. Few
today seek Buddhist truth, and the monasteries
are largely empty. Priests now are mostly igno-
rant and shun *zazen* as a bother; they are dere-

lict in their meditation, concentrating on dec-
orating their temples. Their *zazen* is a sham,
and they are merely masquerading as monks—
the robes they sport will become heavy coats
of torture someday.

Within the cosmos of birth and death, the
taking of life leads to hell; greed leads to rebirth as a hungry ghost; ignorance causes one
to be reborn as an animal; anger turns one into
a demon. Follow the precepts and you attain
rebirth as a human being. Do good deeds and
you ascend to the level of the gods. Above
these six realms there are the four levels of the
Wise Buddhists, altogether ten realms of existence. However, One Thought of Enlightenment reveals them to be formless, with nothing
in between, and not to be loathed, feared, or
desired. Existence is perceived as being nothing
more than a wispy cloud in the vast sky or

foam on the water. No thoughts arise in the mind, so no elements are created. Mind and objects are one and empty, beyond any doubts.

Human birth is like a fire—the father is the flint, the mother is the stone, and the resultant spark is the child. The fire is ignited with the base elements and burns until it exhausts the fuel. The lovemaking between the father and mother produces the spark of life. Since the parents are without beginning, they too flicker out; all things emerge from emptiness—the source of every form. Free yourself from forms and return to the original ground of being. From this ground, life issues forth, but let go of this too.

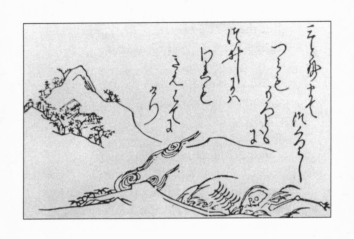

Break open
A cherry tree
And there are no flowers,
But the spring breeze
Brings forth myriad blossoms!

Without a bridge
Clouds climb effortlessly
To heaven;
No need to rely on
Anything Gotama Buddha taught.

Gotama Buddha proclaimed the Dharma for fifty years, and when his disciple Kashyapa asked him for the key to his teaching, Buddha said, "From beginning to end I have not proclaimed a single word," and held up a flower. Kashyapa smiled and Buddha gave him the flower, saying

these words, "You possess the Wondrous Mind of the True Law." "What do you mean?" asked Kashyapa. "My fifty years of preaching," Buddha told him, "has been beckoning to you all the while, just like attracting a child into one's arms with the promise of a reward."

This flower of the Dharma cannot be described in physical, mental, or verbal terms. It is not material or spiritual. It is not intellectual knowledge. Our Dharma is the Flower of the One Vehicle carrying all the Buddhas of the past, present, and future. It holds the twenty-eight Indian and six Chinese patriarchs; it is the original ground of being—all there is. All things are without beginning and are thus all-inclusive. The eight senses, the four seasons, the four great elements (earth, water, fire, wind), all originate in emptiness, but few realize it. Wind is breath, fire is animation, water is blood; when the body is buried or burned it becomes earth. Yet these elements too are without beginning and never abide.

> In this world,
> All things, without exception,
> Are unreal:
> Death itself is
> An illusion.

Delusion makes it appear that though the body dies, the soul endures—this is a grave error. The enlightened declare that both body and soul perish together. "Buddha" is emptiness, and heaven and earth return to the original ground of being. I've set aside the eighty thousand books of scripture and given you the essence in this slim volume. This will bring you great bliss.

Writing something
To leave behind
Is yet another kind of dream:
When I awake I know that
There will be no one to read it.

Notes on the Illustrations

Page ii   Ikkyū gazes at the mountains. From *Ikkyū Shokoku Monogatari Zue,* woodblock print edition issued in 1836.

Page 8   Ikkyū writes a poem on the wall of a samurai manor: "In this world / we must traverse the road of life and death / without assistance; / lonely are we born, / lonely we die." *Ikkyū Shokoku Monogatari Zue.*

Page 15   Ikkyū enjoys the riverbed flowers. *Ikkyū Shokoku Monogatari Zue.*

Page 22   Ikkyū in a mountain hermitage. *Ikkyū Sho-koku Monogatari Zue.*

Page 29   Ikkyū carries about a skull on New Year's Day. From *Ikkyū Banashi,* woodblock print edition of 1668.

Page 36   Ikkyū aids the farmers by writing a petition to their feudal landlord. *Ikkyū Shokoku Monogatari Zue.*

Page 44   Ikkyū fishes for shrimp in a stream. *Ikkyū Shokoku Monogatari Zue.*

Page 50–51   A monk plays the flute while drifting in a boat. *Ikkyū Shokoku Monogatari Zue.*

Page 60   Ikkyū sports beneath the cherry blossoms. *Ikkyū Shokoku Monogatari Zue.*

Page 69   Noh actor. Ikkyū is reputed to have authored several somber Noh dramas. *Ikkyū Shokoku Monogatari Zue.*

Page 79   Ikkyū with a courtesan. *Ikkyū Banashi.*

Page 84   Moonlit night. *Ikkyū Shokoku Monogatari Zue.*

Page 90   Ikkyū as abbot of Daitoku-ji. *Ikkyū Shokoku Monogatari Zue.*

Page 98   The illustrations here and on the following pages are taken from a woodblock edition of *Gaikotsu* printed in 1693.

SHAMBHALA CENTAUR EDITIONS

THE BOOK OF THE HEART
Embracing the Tao
    by Loy Ching-Yuen
        Translated by Trevor Carolan and Bella Chen

DEWDROPS ON A LOTUS LEAF
Zen Poems of Ryokan
        Translated by John Stevens

FOUR HUTS
Asian Writings on the Simple Life
        Translated by Burton Watson

MIDNIGHT FLUTE
Chinese Poems of Love and Longing
        Translated by Sam Hamill

(*Continued on next page*)

PRAYER OF THE HEART
Writings from the *Philokalia*
>Compiled by Saint Nikodimos of the Holy
>Mountain and Saint Makarios of Corinth
>Translated by G. E. H. Palmer, Philip Sherrard,
>and Kallistos Ware

THE SOUND OF WATER
Haiku by Basho, Buson, Issa, and Other Poets
>Translated by Sam Hamill

A STRANGER TO HEAVEN AND EARTH
Poems of Anna Akhmatova
>Translated by Judith Hemschemeyer

THE TALE OF CUPID AND PSYCHE
>by Lucius Apuleius
>Translated by Robert Graves

A TOUCH OF GRACE
Songs of Kabir
>Translated by Linda Hess and Shukdev Singh

WILD WAYS
Zen Poems of Ikkyū
   Translated by John Stevens